My heart pounded as the policewoman took me upstairs in the elevator. The police officers were standing in the open doorway of Simon's room. He was in there, sitting on the bed in vest and pants, self-assured even in that stupid situation.

"There he is!" I cried. Simon looked at me slowly, with contemptuous, bleak eyes. "Who are you?" he demanded.

I almost went berserk. I think it was then that I knew, with a hopeless certainty, that I was in really big trouble.

FREED
FOR
LIFE

RITA NIGHTINGALE
with David Porter

LIVING BOOKS
Tyndale House Publishers, Inc.
Wheaton, Illinois

First Living Books edition, April 1983
Tyndale House Publishers, Inc., Wheaton, Illinois.

This United States edition is produced by
arrangement with the original publisher,
Marshall Morgan & Scott, London, England.

Printed in the United States of America.

To

MOTHER & DAD

and

my two very special sisters,

ANN & JUNE

for their love, courage, and devotion

Contents

Foreword

"So, who is Rita Nightingale?" I remember asking my associate the first time he told me the story of the young British girl in a Thailand prison. Prayer groups seemed to be springing up all over the world for her.

"I mean, why all the fuss?" I persisted. Sure, it was a tragic case: young girl on a pleasure jaunt meets glamorous boyfriend and then is "set up"; the police find bags of heroin in the false bottom of the suitcase her boyfriend gave her; and the Thai courts throw the book at her, twenty years caged in an Oriental prison. I had heard of hundreds of other cases like hers. We receive mail almost every day from Americans caught in prisons around the world: no friends, no money, unable to speak the language.

Indeed as the facts emerged, we learned there was much that was unusual about Rita Nightingale's case. We received letters from two missionaries who had visited her, giving an exciting account of her dramatic conversion to Christ. Then some Christian lawyers in Australia wrote me with a full account of her case. Government officials in England, I soon discovered, were interested in her case; there was even discussion in the House of Commons. Newspapers were writing extensively about her. And everywhere I heard about people praying for her. I came to realize that God must be doing something very special through her life in that faraway jail.

My close friend, Fred Rhodes, who had helped start Prison Fellowship with me, tried to see Rita when he was in Bangkok attending some Baptist meetings. He arrived at the gates of the Lard Yao Prison, but after a long wait, the officials refused to let him inside. He, nevertheless, brought back an appalling description of the place: open sewers, heat, insects, and stench.

Over the next months, several other Christian friends tried to get inside the prison. Each one was rebuffed. Then Kathryn Grant, a missionary in the Orient for twenty years and now vice-president of our ministry for international affairs, persisted. Finally in November of 1979, through some nearly miraculous circumstances, she succeeded. Kathryn was able to meet alone with Rita, and then again with all of the other Western female prisoners.

It was Rita's spirit—her warmth and radiance—that so impressed Kathryn. Kathryn wrote to me at the time of her visit:

Rita is beautiful, with soft brown wavy hair, lovely warm complexion, a very soft person, extremely refined, cautious, no coarseness. You would think if you met her that she was just a lovely young Christian girl going to church. And joyous. To feel that joy, you'd have to see what conditions they're living under. No American or Westerner can conceive of the living conditions. The heat! No screens . . . an incredible diet . . . yet over and over, Rita was saying, "You know, all of my bitterness is gone. I don't ask questions anymore. I just say, 'Thank you, Lord, for what you've done.'"

Kathryn's report went on to describe how Rita had promised the Lord that the minute she was set free, she would go back to start working in the prisons, bringing the hope of the gospel to others.

It was obvious then that God was grooming and training this young British girl for something big and important. Yet, what could it be? She had nearly seventeen years remaining on her twenty-year sentence. So we continued to pray for Rita as did hundreds, perhaps thousands, of Christians around the world who were part of the prayer chains. But our hopes dimmed as the months passed. Government officials who worked on her case held out little hope.

It was as if God had to show us that all our efforts would be in vain, that the situation was humanly impossible, before he would release her from prison. Only when we came to the end of our own efforts would we be able to see the magnificent working of our sovereign God. It was divine intervention that ultimately set this young Lancashire girl free.

The story you are about to read is thrilling, gripping, and at times frightening. But it is more than the story of one woman's nightmarish ordeal in a faraway continent. It is a story of how God reaches into the lives of ordinary people, sometimes using the most extraordinary means to raise up those he calls for his purpose. Ironically, it often happens that a prison cell is his testing ground. It was for Joseph, for Jeremiah, for Paul, Peter, and in modern times, for Dietrich Bonhoeffer and Alexander Solzhenitsyn. And now for Rita Nightingale.

The message of this book goes far beyond the thrilling adventures of this young British girl. There is in Rita's experience the most profound and prophetic challenge to our materialistic Western culture. Solzhenitsyn summed it up beautifully when he was writing from the Gulag: "Bless you, prison, for having been in my life." For it was there lying on rotting prison straw that he learned that "the meaning of earthly existence lies not, as we have grown used to thinking, in prospering, but in the development of the soul."

God used prison to reverse the course of my life. I could not forget what I had seen and what I had lived with, and so I began to return again and again. That was the beginning of Prison Fellowship, a ministry now reaching out to inmates all around the globe. God put the same call on Rita Nightingale, and I am proud to have her as my co-worker and colleague in this ministry.

Be prepared as you read on. For the One who called this young girl to his service through the remarkable chain of events described in this book may put a call on your life as well.

Charles W. Colson

Preface

In working with Rita on her story, I have been helped by a large number of individuals and organizations. I am especially grateful to the editor of the *Lancashire Evening Telegraph,* who made available to me the newspaper's unique archive of material concerning the case, and to David Allin, news editor of the same newspaper, whose articles over three years played a major part in maintaining public awareness of Rita's plight. I had also been given access to family papers, letters, and other documents by the Nightingale family.

Acknowledgment is gratefully made to Dr. Ann England; Mr. Peter Elsom; Mrs. Jane Winter; Mrs. Daphne Boddington; my wife, Tricia; and a number of others who kindly read the manuscript. Technical help has been supplied by Mr. Ken Davies. I have made use of a large number of books, including Apa production's encyclopedic Insight Guides, and have been given assistance by the Hong Kong

Government offices and several London embassies. Any faults in the book cannot be laid at the door of any of the foregoing, nor can the help given by official agencies be interpreted as an endorsement by any government of the views expressed.

All names have been changed with the exception of family and close friends. In general, names in common use have been substituted. It is regretted if unintentional embarrassment is thereby caused to individuals happening to bear these names.

David Porter

The facts recorded in this book are true to the best of my knowledge, and the opinions expressed are honestly held.

Rita Nightingale

1 Bangkok

All foreign visitors entering Thailand must be in possession of a passport . . . endorsed and valid for Thailand. As a general rule, all foreign nationals are required to apply for and obtain visas from Thai Embassies or Consulates abroad. Every kind of visa is valid for a 90-day period from the date of issue. Customs regulations: prohibited items. All kinds of narcotics—hemp, opium, cocaine, morphine, heroin; obscene literature, pictures or articles.

Thailand in brief, Public Relations Department, Government of Thailand

I ran a finger around my neck, easing the damp collar of my blouse. Reaching for my handbag, I extracted my powder compact, opened it, and peered at my reflection in the tiny mirror. My nose was getting shiny again. I squinted sideways and applied the powderpuff until I was satisfied.

Holding the mirror further away, I inspected myself and nodded complacently. I was looking good. My short dark hair framed a face which, with its well-defined cheekbones and almost slanted eyes, had sometimes been mistaken for that of an Asian girl. I always took a lot of trouble over my looks. My lipstick was just right, and my eyeshadow had that casual look which takes half an hour in front of a mirror to achieve.

I snapped the compact shut, slipped it back into my bag, and wriggled myself into a more comfortable position. The air-conditioned departure lounge was cooler than the remorseless Bangkok heat outside, but it was packed with people and the heat was becoming oppressive.

Ready for the chill of Paris in March, I'd packed warm clothes when I'd left Hong Kong. I smiled at the thought, as I glanced down at my expensive white silk suit and the smart high heels I'd kicked off. Above and around the milling passengers, impersonal loudspeaker voices in Thai and English announced arrivals and departures. Soon the Paris flight would be called.

My baggage had been checked in, and I had nothing to do but kill time. I fanned myself lazily with a magazine. Nearby, a couple of Europeans were playing cards; watching them out of the corner of her eye was an incredibly beautiful Thai girl. I felt myself becoming drowsy.

Somebody was tapping my shoulder. I jerked myself awake. A Thai airport official, coolly immaculate in slacks and a crisp white shirt, stood looking down at me.

"Miss Nightingale?" he asked quietly. "I am from the Customs Department. Please come with me."

"I beg your pardon? What? . . . "

"You must come with me, please."

His voice was neutral, his expression inscrutable. I didn't know what he could possibly want, and I wasn't much bothered; I just hoped it wouldn't take too long to sort out. It was almost time for my flight. Irritated, I picked up my handbag and radio and went with the official.

He escorted me to an office. Several customs staff looked up as I entered. Something about their manner gave me a sinking feeling inside; this was one of those official holdups, a piece of red tape that was going to take time to go through. *They won't hold the Paris flight for me,* I thought and cursed my luck. Delayed in a random customs check a quarter of an hour before leaving! *At least there isn't anything that they can arrest me for,* I thought cynically.

Even when the officials demanded my passport and plane tickets, I still thought it was a routine check. Everybody was speaking Thai; I couldn't understand what was happening. When I asked what was going on and why I was being detained, they wouldn't say directly. One of them gave me a strange look and asked, "What do you know about heroin?" I laughed, still thinking they were going through the usual formulas. Then one of them reached for my passport and cancelled my departure visa. I stopped laughing. Whatever was going on was serious.

The Paris flight had long departed. I was still in a Don Muang Airport customs office. It was about half past ten at night. I was taken to another room where there were about ten customs officers. There was also a young Chinese man sitting apart from the others, nervously twining and untwining his fingers. He was watching everything that was going on, his eyes as hard as flint.

My bags were on a long trestle table. As I watched, the officials began to unpack them systematically. I smiled, knowing they were on a wild goose chase. They took each item out, shaking it or feeling it with probing fingers. I watched scornfully as the pile of garments and other possessions mounted up. As the last odds and ends were taken from the bags, examined, and placed on the pile, my smile broadened.

A moment later the smile was gone again. One of the officials was still exploring the empty bag. He stood it on end and felt around inside, grunting with satisfaction as he withdrew a large, flat leather-covered board. Discarding it, he delved deeper and began to pull out heavy plastic bags. The holdalls had been fitted with false bottoms.

I began to tremble. There hadn't been any false bottoms in them when I'd packed them in Hong Kong. Incredulously, I saw packages of pinkish brown stuff being pulled from my luggage. I'd never seen them before. The official showed them to his colleague: the other bag was examined. It had a false bottom too.

Some of the bystanders remarked, "Heroin!" in pleased voices, as if they had hoped for such a discovery. I felt sick. So that was what was in the packages. I'd smoked marijuana, but had never had anything to do with hard drugs. I always thought it was a white powder, but this was more like brown sugar.

There was pandemonium. Several of the officials watching were clearly delighted at the discovery; it seemed that I was quite a catch. They joked and laughed among themselves. Somebody shouted at me in English, "You like heroin? They shoot you— they give you thirty years! Ha ha!"

People were coming in and out, staring and pointing. By now there were police officers in the room, watching the proceedings. They wore the normal uniform—slacks and short-sleeved military shirt given a touch of formality by the hard-peaked police cap and the efficient leather belt to hold a handgun and ammunition. I'd passed such men scores of times in the last few days without giving them a second glance; now I avoided looking at their weapons. Some of the uniformed men were carrying machine guns.

The guns made a bizarre and frightening contrast to the carnival atmosphere of the room. I noticed that one of the officers, for no apparent reason, was wearing a shirt decorated with Mickey Mouse cartoons. Nearby, somebody was making a video film of the whole thing; several photographers were present. I tried to hide myself behind a cardigan when I saw the cameras pointed at me, but I couldn't avoid them all.

For some reason, I don't know why, there were children in the room, laughing and giggling at me. The officials even turned my radio cassette player on, but they weren't satisfied when it proved to be working; they proceeded to pull the back off. To my horror I saw that one of the loudspeakers had been removed. In its place was more of the brown stuff.

I couldn't cry at first. I was completely numb. Then the numbness gave way to blazing anger, and I did cry—great, gulping, angry sobs. I wanted somebody to go out and get the guy who had set me up for all this. "Simon . . . Simon, . . ." I muttered, over and over. It must have been Simon. Of course, I saw it all now; they should look for Simon, I insisted. He was still at the hotel, as far as I knew. But I couldn't make anybody understand.

I was taken to another room. A woman officer ordered me to remove my clothes. I was searched efficiently and without comment, the way an animal might be searched for parasites. The fright and degradation only intensified the feeling, taking root in me, that this was some sort of weird nightmare, that in a few moments I would wake up.

All told, this ordeal went on for another three hours.

Repeatedly, a document was placed before me, an official form on government paper filled out in the elaborate Thai script. I couldn't understand it. "What is it?" I demanded.

"It's a formality; it's nothing. It says that these things were found in your possession when you were attempting to leave the country. It's a formality. You must sign it." A pen was jabbed at the place where I was to sign.

I refused. I vigorously refused several times. Eventually a police captain arrived. He was calm and reasonable. Even the sight of his uniform was reassuring; he was clearly a senior officer, and would take charge of this circus and sort everything out.

He sat down and looked at me thoughtfully. "Now. Tell me exactly what has happened."

"Can't we go somewhere quiet to talk?" I pleaded. I just wanted to fit the pieces together, to find out what was going on. He agreed and took me to a bare, cell-like room, lit by a single harsh unshaded bulb. We sat down. He took a notebook and pencil from his shirt pocket and placed them on the desk in front of him.

"You must find Simon," I said desperately. "Simon will know what this is all about."

The captain scribbled. "Your boyfriend?"

"No, not my boyfriend—James is my boyfriend, James Wong. He's meeting me in Paris; that's where I'm supposed to be." Inwardly, I shuddered and wondered how long it would be before I got there. "Simon—Simon Lo—he's the guy I traveled to Bangkok with," I persisted. "He had my bags in his room. It must have been him."

He stared at me impassively, waiting for me to continue. I stumbled on.

"We were staying at the Asia Hotel. I checked out from there today. He must still be there. I know he is."

He smiled skeptically.

"He must be!" I said angrily. "He was there when

he said good-bye to me—he put me in a taxi there. Why don't you go and arrest him?"

The captain tapped his pencil on the desk and deliberated. Then he left the room, and I heard him talking to the customs officials in the corridor. When he returned, he nodded brusquely. "You will come with us to the hotel." It was an order, not a request. I was relieved and excited. Simon wasn't going to get away with it. It was going to be all right; soon I would be on my way to Paris.

By now it was early morning. The captain, another policeman, and two policewomen escorted me. There was little conversation. We went in two police cars to the Asia Hotel in the silence of the curfew: martial law was then operating in Thailand. Dawn was just breaking. The gilded temples and lush tropical trees lining the empty streets appeared through a drizzling mist. I paid little attention to them. The driver stared at the road ahead, occasionally exchanging a comment in Thai with one of his colleagues. A policewoman by my side, I sat hunched up in the back of the car, wanting it all to be over.

The hotel gates were locked. We waited grimly for somebody to come down and open them. One of the policewomen waited with me in the reception area while the others went upstairs. After a few minutes the captain rang down to say I was to be taken upstairs. My heart pounded as we stood in the elevator.

The police officers were standing in the open doorway of Simon's room. He was in there, sitting on the bed in vest and pants, self-assured even in that stupid situation. He looked up as I arrived.

"There he is!" I cried. Simon looked at me slowly, with contemptuous, bleak eyes.

"Who are you?" he demanded.

I almost went berserk. I think it was then that I knew, with a hopeless certainty, that I was in really big trouble.

2 Australia

*We went to Tarronga Zoo last week
and it was fabulous . . . the things
I liked best were the Koala bears
and baby kangaroos. . . .*

*I've got in a bit of a rut here. It's all
work and watching telly or reading.
I'm reading between five and six
books a week. I haven't got much
interest in anything, so it's time I got
out for a while. . . .*

*After a while Carl and I became more
than friends. Nudge, nudge, wink-
wink, say no more!!!*

*Don't worry, Mother, if I get into any
trouble you'll hear about it. . . .*

Letters home, 1976

Travel was in my blood. It was a fever I had had since childhood. My father, Harry Nightingale, had traveled the Far East as a regular soldier before the war and had loved the people and places he had seen. He used to tell me and my two sisters that the world was large and exciting. He urged us to travel as soon as we were old enough. "The world's a bigger place than Blackburn," he said. I loved travel and enjoyed being a stranger, someone from far-away. When I thought of my old friends in England, I pitied them. They were stuck back there, and I was in the exotic East, living the glamorous life I'd always dreamed of.

My home town, Blackburn, was an industrial town in the north of England set among windswept moors and the foothills of the Pennines. We were, and are, a close-knit family. We lived in an apartment above the Stokers Arms, the pub my parents ran. When I left school, I did a term's prenursing course at a local college, and then started work as a cadet nurse at Queen's Park Hospital, Blackburn. I hoped to become a State Registered Nurse, but I never completed my training.

It looked as though I was going to spend my life in Blackburn, close to my family, working in the town's hospital. My mother had to run the pub nearly singlehanded; Dad was seriously ill upstairs. I and my sisters helped out there when we could.

Though there was much to be done, there was time for a social life as well. I met John, a tall, lean blond boy from Stockport. We began to see each other regularly. I was fascinated by him. He had traveled, through Europe to Greece and on to Israel. He had the glamour I was looking for; he could tell stories of foreign countries. His friends were travelers; they mostly lived in the Lake District. It was a different set from the one I'd known in Blackburn. None of them had much money, but that was part of the fascination.

We talked about our dreams of traveling, and our frustration at the cramped surroundings of Blackburn. Our friendship grew and developed into something more serious. I was seventeen; I thought I knew it all. I gave up my job and married John against everybody's advice. The wedding was overshadowed by the forebodings of relatives and the knowledge that Dad, who was too ill to attend, was dying. His funeral followed our wedding by only a few weeks. Nine months later I left Blackburn with John. We were bound for Sydney, Australia. A new life, a new world.

I loved Australia. At first we lived in Sydney, where we soon lost our English pallor. We surfed and swam. We ate prawns and other delicious food. We spent our free time lazing on Bondi Beach, which I'd heard about in England and promised myself I'd see one day. John was unemployed, but I picked up enough work for us to scrape by. You could have said I was happy, but in reality I was confused and mixed up. Only months after arriving in Sydney, I was really miserable.

For a start, I was terribly homesick. I would never have left Blackburn if I hadn't married—I loved my family too much. Hardly a day went by without wistful thoughts of Mother and my sisters, aunts and uncles, and the pub on the street corner in the center of Blackburn.

Also our marriage was going wrong. Daily, in a

hundred little ways, John and I were drifting apart. We didn't talk about it to each other—we spent most of our time together arguing—but I didn't need to be told that things weren't working out. I was resentful that I had to go out to work while John mostly stayed at home. Even our first anniversary was marked by a huge argument. I was beginning to realize that my determination to stand on my own two feet and to see the world hadn't solved the frustration I'd felt in England. My new marriage, my new start, was falling apart already, and I knew it was more my fault than John's. What had started as a teenage love affair fed on dreams of travel wasn't strong enough to survive our growing up. There didn't seem much I could do to alter matters, and to be honest, I didn't try very hard.

Perhaps a change of surroundings would help. We moved to Adelaide, and from there we decided to go north, hitchhiking to Darwin through the outback. It was the sort of adventure we'd talked of back in England, when we'd planned and dreamed of the things we were going to do. The reality wasn't glamorous. We fought and hurt each other all the way north. When we finally arrived in Darwin and settled in a caravan park, I knew that it was the end. One day I wrote a note for John when I left for work. I said I didn't want him anymore. He was still asleep. I left the note on the table and walked out of our flat and out of our marriage. It had lasted six months after our emigration.

John went back to England, and I was alone in Australia. My family urged me to come home too. I almost did, but in the end decided to stay on. Traveling had left me restless and unsatisfied. I wanted to settle down, get my life together, and have somebody care for me. I wanted love and affection.

I hadn't much time to get lonely, however. I moved to the Darwin YWCA, got a job as a barmaid, and made scores of friends, throwing myself into a hectic social whirl. I told myself I was having a great time. Before long I was going out with Bernie, a curly-headed, bronzed Lancashire man I'd met in the bar where I worked. He was attractive, kind, and had a wonderful sense of humor. We grew very close; soon we were lovers. One day we were laughing at something when he suddenly fell silent.

"What's up?" I demanded.

He looked at me speculatively. "Ever thought of getting married again?"

I shrugged. "Once bitten! . . ." I countered flippantly, and changed the subject.

He didn't raise the matter again, and I certainly didn't want to remind him.

After a few months I left the YWCA, and moved in with him. I was able to convince myself I was happy, at least for most of the time. I began to feel things for him I'd never felt for John. Sometimes it seemed that I was happier then than I'd ever been before. But I had come to Australia with the idea that after two years I would go back home to visit my family. Even when I was living with Bernie, this idea persisted. Bernie, who'd made the trip himself several years before, understood how I felt. In 1974, after being in Australia for just under two years, I left. Bernie was going to follow in a few months. By then, we'd begun to talk of marriage.

I planned to be in England for my twenty-first

birthday. Shirley, an English friend in the lawyer's office where I was working, wanted to go home too. We decided we would travel to England overland. We flew from Darwin up to Bali, then traveled through Java and Sumatra and over to Penang in Malaysia. From Penang we went to Singapore and up the east coast to Thailand and Bangkok. There we seized the opportunity to take a cheap flight to Hong Kong, where we stayed six weeks intending to return to Bangkok and go on to Nepal.

One morning I was sitting at breakfast in our Hong Kong lodgings, opening some mail that had been waiting for me. I finished reading, groaned, and sat back in my chair. Shirley looked up.

"Problems?"

I pointed to the letters. "From my sisters. Trouble at home. Mother's been having some problems with the pub." Chinese music from a transistor radio below floated up through the open window, mingling with the traffic noises and the perpetual babble of conversation in the streets. Another hot Hong Kong day. Sightseeing, shopping, perhaps a trip out to the countryside. It was enticing.

"What do you want to do today?" asked Shirley. A wave of homesickness swept over me. I made up my mind.

"I'm going home, Shirley. By plane. Tonight."

I arrived in England the next day. At first I worked with my mother, but I found it very difficult to settle down in the job. A pub is almost a twenty-four hour commitment, and after my travels I couldn't cope with the lunchtime, suppertime, and evening work, day after day. I daydreamed a lot about Australia and Southeast Asia, comparing the glamour of those places with the routine of the pub.

It takes a lot of grace to live and work with somebody, and soon I had a falling-out with my mother. To add to my confusion, Bernie arrived in England and proposed. But he had been delayed by the cyclone which devastated Darwin that year, and it was twelve months since I'd seen him. In the interim I had become confused again. I couldn't work out what I wanted from life, and his visit wasn't a happy time for either of us. In the end he went back to Australia without me, and things got so tense between me and my mother that I decided I would have to stop working at home. I went back to Blackburn Hospital where I enrolled as an auxiliary nurse.

I stayed there for several months, working nights. But once again I found it impossible to submit to the discipline of a regular and well-ordered life. The hospital seemed to be closing around me like a prison, trapping me. Gradually, I began to make plans to leave home again.

My family would have liked me to stay. My mother needed me, but more than that she had the fears and worries of any mother seeing her daughter going abroad. Years later she told a reporter: "It would have been easy to say, 'Don't travel—it will worry me to death.' But you just can't do that to your kids, can you?" So she wished me well and even lent me money to supplement the several hundred dollars I'd saved.

I traveled back with Bernie's sister, Pauline. We spent a few weeks in Singapore and then arrived in Darwin. Pauline and I stayed at Bernie's place, but I found it impossible to pick up the threads again. I needed time to sort out my feelings. I slept alone. It wasn't sex I needed. I wanted to sort out my head about whether I loved this man enough to settle down for life.

Our relationship deteriorated. Once again, I found myself unable to change things. I saw the danger signs, but was powerless to do anything about them. Twenty miles out of town, with no car, I was living in the house of a man I couldn't decide to marry. I didn't know what I wanted anymore.

I moved to a government hostel, bought myself a motorbike, and made a number of friends. But I was so unsettled. For me, Darwin was Bernie; and things were bad between us, and it was my fault. Everywhere I went in Darwin reminded me of him. I stuck it out for nearly a year, until finally I said to myself, *What you need, Rita Nightingale, is a little break.*

I made my plans. I would take a few months off and travel again. I would clear my head, think things through, and hopefully come to some decisions. And I would take the same route that I had traveled with Shirley. This time I would go alone.

In Bali, I met Carl, a funny, outrageous guy who was good to be with. We traveled together for a while, sharing my motorbike and his sleeping bag. At Bangkok, he left for England. He wanted me to go with him. He was a great companion. I'd had a wonderful time with him, but he was a distraction. I was traveling in order to sort myself out, to find out what I wanted from life, to think about Bernie, about home, about the future. I was unhappy and I knew that something was missing, yet I didn't know what it was. Certainly the last thing I was looking for was yet another heavy relationship to get involved in.

And so late in 1976 Carl and I said good-bye at Bangkok Airport. He went back to London, and I flew to Hong Kong.

3   Hong Kong

It's girls that one goes to a place like the Kokusai for, and the Kokusai has plenty of them, all very attractive and all very accommodating. . . . A hostess can set you back HK$15 for every 15 minutes you're trying to make conversation with her. No problem buying a hostess out, but that'll set you back a lot more dollars.

Tobin's Guide to Hong Kong Nightlife, by Anthony L. Tobin

I arrived in Hong Kong a few days before Christmas with Sue, a girl I'd met in Java. She'd been on the same plane. I caught my breath as we walked to Nathan Road from Kai Tak Airport. The excitement

I'd felt when I had last been to the Colony was back.

High above us, hanging from the towering buildings and festooned across the street were thousands of bright blue, scarlet, and white signs and advertisements in bold Chinese calligraphy. At street level, the shops open to the pavement were packed with tourists, deliberating over displays of everything in the world that one might want to buy. Impatient crowds pushed past as I drank in the spectacle: the roar of traffic forcing its way down the street, people of all nationalities thronging the pavements, Chinese music blaring from loudspeakers in shop doorways. A magical, shimmering view of the harbor was just visible beyond it all at the end of the thoroughfare. A mixture of traffic fumes, cooking smells, and the occasional whiff of fish from the harbor pervaded the air. Over everything a mist blurred the tops of buildings and obscured the view of the harbor.

"This way!" I said to Sue, my voice raised against the noise. I'd met up with her on the plane from Bangkok. I already knew her—we'd met in Bali—and we'd decided to team up in Hong Kong for a while.

We made our way down Nathan Road, stopping to gaze at shop windows piled with jewelry, calculators, cameras, and other luxuries. Even the voices of passersby grumbling at us were an exotic mixture of languages. I loved it. It was what travel was all about, as far as I was concerned; and my own delight was doubled by witnessing that of Sue, who hadn't been to Hong Kong before.

At its harbor end, Nathan Road becomes the "Golden Mile," where nightclubs, bars, and hotels jostle the large shops. I indicated a side road, and we turned down a crowded alley. "Chungking," I announced, as we stopped in front of a shabby, sprawling tenement block of enormous size. Sue looked up at it doubtfully. "This is it?" she said. I laughed. "This is Chungking Mansions."

I'd stayed at Chungking when I was last in Hong Kong. A conglomeration of lodging houses, shops, and cheap eating houses, the whole thing forms one of the larger blocks in Nathan Road. We wanted cheap accommodations, and Chungking was certainly cheap; you got what you paid for. I'd told Sue about it and she had been enthusiastic. Now that we were there, she hovered uncertainly.

"The Hilton's quite near, if you'd prefer," I teased, pointing back toward Nathan Road. Sue grinned.

"In for a penny. . . ."

We entered the block by way of a courtyard filled with different shops and a number of elevators. A bulletin board was placed at each elevator entrance. We scanned the scraps of paper and picked an apartment which seemed reasonably priced.

A middle-aged Chinese in an undershirt and shorts was sitting on a balcony and announced himself as the landlord of the apartment. He seemed supremely uninterested in doing business, but eventually we managed to persuade him to rent us the apartment. "You pay rent in advance," he emphasized.

"That's fine," we said. He extended a hand for the money.

I kept my hands in my pockets. "We'd like to see the room first."

He scowled. "Why you want to see room? It's

37

room. That's what you want, isn't it? Maybe you don't want room."

He turned his back and studied the courtyard below. It took us several minutes of further bargaining before he reluctantly took us to the apartment.

It was small and uncarpeted. Two single beds, a chest of drawers, and a dilapidated wardrobe took up most of the available space. By Chungking standards, it was quite pleasant, and possessed a window—a real luxury in Chungking—from which there was an impressive view of the back of another wing of the Mansions. Sue and I looked at each other, smiled happily, and paid the landlord. Thrusting the cash into his pocket, he shuffled away down the corridor, complaining bitterly under his breath.

We dumped our knapsacks, put our belongings away, and went out to explore.

"What first?" I asked.

"Food!" cried Sue. "I'm starving!" So was I.

We found a small Chinese restaurant, where we sampled the exotic delights of the menu. We ate until we could eat no more, and then sat and watched Hong Kong go by until we felt ready to move again.

It was mid-evening. A slight evening chill offset the sultry heat as the sky darkened into night. The neon signs were lit along Nathan Road, thousands of them. Sue wanted to explore on her own, and I had a number of things I wanted to do, so we agreed to split up. I stood in the street and planned my evening. Should I go down to the harbor or wander about the shops along Nathan Road, which was becoming even brighter as the neon signs glowed and colorful Chinese lanterns appeared in the restaurant windows? It was all so exciting; the familiar thrill was very strong. It was good to be back. I decided first of all to see whether any of the people I'd known last time were still around. I'd been quite friendly with a girl called Robin, who worked at the Kokusai nightclub on Nathan Road near Chungking. I wanted to see her again. I set off for the Kokusai.

The entrance, like those of most of the better-class clubs, was a discreet doorway. I peered in. The reception lounge was deserted. Nobody was around; it was nine o'clock—still early for the club to be open. The turbanned doorkeeper I remembered was nowhere to be seen. I went to the back entrance and pushed the door open. Framed color photographs of the dance floor, the hostesses, and the band lined an expensively carpeted staircase leading down to the Kokusai.

Downstairs, the empty club looked drab and unused. The lighting was harsh and revealing, and the mirrors which lined the walls reflected empty seats and tables. The bandstand was deserted. A barman behind a tiny bar was polishing glasses, slowly and with an air of boredom. A smell of stale tobacco smoke hung in the air.

A Eurasian girl was sitting at a table reading a magazine. She looked up. "Want something?"

"Is Robin here?" I asked.

She shook her head and turned a page. "No, she doesn't work here anymore. You know her?"

"Not really," I said. "I just got to know her a bit when I was last here."

She closed her magazine. She seemed eager for a chat. "Cathy took Robin's job. She's here. Do you know Cathy?"

"Cathy? I don't think. . . ."

"Oh, she's great!" said the girl. "You'll like her. Come and say hello to Cathy."

She seized my arm and took me through to the hostesses' dressing room, where I had sometimes called to meet Robin. It was as I remembered it. Two or three girls were sitting at the long row of mirrors, putting on makeup and doing their hair. Lipsticks and jars of face cream were strewn along the bench, and expensive dresses were tossed casually over the backs of chairs.

A pretty, dark-haired girl in a kimono was delving into a pile of clothes. "Mary Rose!" she shouted sulkily as we entered. "Where's my slip? You've dumped all your things on top of mine. . . ."

She stopped short as she saw us.

"Hi! Who are you?"

"She's looking for Robin, Cathy."

Cathy inspected me. "Robin's left here. Move some things and grab a seat while I get myself sorted out. Just flown in?"

I liked Cathy immediately. We got into conversation, and I told her about my travels and my previous visit to Hong Kong. She introduced me to the other girls. One of them reached out a hand and touched my face. "You look so fresh!" she said. It was true. I was wearing no makeup, and I'd been traveling in the sunshine for several weeks. These girls worked for months on end without seeing much daylight.

After a while Cathy asked, "How long are you going to be in Hong Kong? Do you want a job?"

It wasn't something I'd given much thought to. "What sort of job?"

"Here. You could be a hostess."

"What does a hostess do?"

"You entertain people—sit with them when they come in the club . . . dance with them, let them buy you drinks, maybe other things, you know? That's up to you. It's a good job. You'd enjoy it."

"No," I said. "I don't want to be a hostess."

Cathy hesitated and dropped her voice, looking at me shrewdly. "You needn't tell anybody, but I'm leaving here soon. I haven't told them yet. You could have my job. I'm a receptionist here."

Through having known Robin I knew what receptionists did. It was a glamorous life. You greeted people when they came in, looked after them, assigned them a hostess, and kept them company only as long as you wanted to.

It didn't take me long to decide. "Yes," I said. "I wouldn't mind."

By midnight each night the Kokusai was transformed. There were red roses on each table, and lamps with crimson shades, which made intimate alcoves of light where visitors sat with their friends or with a club hostess. The small dance floor was usually full of couples dancing to the Filipino band.

The job was marvelous. I couldn't believe my luck. It wasn't like work at all. I'd always enjoyed having a good time, I liked parties and dancing, and I'd missed them on my travels. For the first few nights I simply enjoyed being there, smiling happily at people and making them welcome. Then one night Cathy said to me, "Come on, I want you to meet someone; he's a really nice guy." He was a good-looking German. He beamed at me.

"Rita. That is a nice name. So. You would like to dance?"

I was more than happy to dance with him, sit with him at his table, and generally look after him. It was like any evening spent with a pleasant companion. After an hour or two I suddenly thought, *Well, I guess this is supposed to be what I'm paid for!* I always found it difficult to think of visitors as "work," and I certainly enjoyed being paid to have a nice time. In fact the only visitors I didn't get on with were known and disliked by all of us—the hard drinkers, loud talkers, and clumsy gropers; most of the girls flatly refused to sit with them. So did I after a few experiences, including the occasion when one of them pawed me furtively on the dance floor. I managed to throw him off balance, and he ended up sprawled among the band.

The Kokusai wasn't like some Hong Kong nightclubs which are notorious pickup places, where the girls are prostitutes in all but name. Some of the girls from the Kokusai were using the club as a base for prostitution, but not all. Officially, the club's policy was clear: any such arrangements made between a visitor and a hostess were nothing to do with the club. Girls could be entertained away from the premises by arrangement with the management, but the fee charged was on the basis that the girl was going merely as an escort. I found myself attending some very grand balls and banquets myself, escorting wealthy visitors who needed a companion.

Quite a few of the visitors to the Kokusai made it obvious that they were interested in rather more than dancing and conversation. I was invited back to hotel rooms many times, and became skilled in avoiding such suggestions. I had no moral objections; I'd slept with several boyfriends in the past. But I hated the idea of being bought, of having my availability taken for granted. Sex was something for relationships, not for one-night stands. In any case, most of the men were much older than I. I didn't fancy them anyway. Some of the girls who slept with any customer willing to pay for it thought I was arrogant or at best stupid. One evening one of the girls beckoned me to a quiet corner. She nodded in the direction of one of the customers.

"That guy—see him?" She giggled. "He wants to take you out."

I looked across at him. He was a well-dressed, middle-aged man. I recognized him. He saw me looking and confidently smiled back. I stared at him coldly; he winked and waved a hand. "Oh, he does, does he?" I retorted. "Well, I'm not going."

"But—he's a movie star!"

"I don't care what he is," I snapped. "I know what he wants and he's not getting it. I'm not going."

That night, in the dressing room, one of the Chinese girls stormed in. She threw her things onto the floor and marched up to me. "Who do you think you are?" she demanded, furiously. "You think you're better than the rest of us? You think you've got something special?"

I was fumbling for a reply when another Chinese girl defended me in a torrent of scathing Chinese, and the first girl retreated, glaring at me and swearing fluently. Later, my protector advised me, "Don't be pushed around, Rita; don't ever let them push you. I've worked here for fifteen years, and I've never slept with anybody for money. So don't let them tell you you've got to. You don't."

Cathy became a good friend and was very kind to me. On my first day, when I told her I had no nice clothes to wear in the club, she lent me one of her own beautiful dresses. Later, she asked me where I was staying. When I told her, she wrinkled her nose expressively.

"We've got space in our apartment," she said thoughtfully. She and her husband lived in an attractive block not far from the Kokusai. "You could come and bring Sue."

We leaped at the chance to have our own rooms, with television and the use of a kitchen. We had been at Chungking for only a few days, and we left without regrets.

Sue worked at the Kokusai too for a while, but her tall frame and boisterous American humor didn't adapt well. She soon left and found a job at a Wild West saloon where she was a great success.

Cathy left the Kokusai, as she had intended, a short time after I arrived. She also left the apartment, and her husband. She went to live with her lover in his hotel. Sue and I stayed on in the apartment, and so did Cathy's husband. One night, we were sitting chatting in my room, when he suddenly leaned over and grasped my hands.

"Sleep with me tonight, Rita," he pleaded. "I need to hold somebody again."

"Oh, get away!" I scoffed. "Go down to Wanchai and find yourself a woman!"

He let go of my hands, a hurt expression in his

eyes, and left the room; he never referred to the matter again.

The weeks I'd intended to stay in Hong Kong lengthened into months. I was glad to be earning money, and it was a good life, the sort of life I'd always dreamed of. But when I was on my own, I sometimes found myself depressed and discontented. I couldn't put my finger on the reason. It was strange, I thought. How could anybody be having this good a time, and not be happy?

4 James

Dear Mother,

*Well, what a mess I've got myself
into. Make no mistake—it's very
serious. I shall start from the very
beginning. . . .*

Letter home, April 19, 1977

Two men appeared at the Kokusai at the time of the
Chinese New Year. They stood chatting with one of
the receptionists. I recognized one of them; he was a
regular, the star of many kung fu films. I'd spent
whole afternoons watching matinee films, in Chinese
with English subtitles, and I adored them. He had
starred in several of my favorites. I'd gotten used to
seeing him at the Kokusai.

I didn't recognize his companion, but I liked what I saw. *Wow!* I said to myself. *He's some guy!* He certainly was. James Wong was taller than most Chinese men, twenty-seven, very good-looking, and very, very smooth. He was beautifully dressed too: white suit, silk shirt. I couldn't take my eyes off him, and when he asked me to go over and sit with him, I went like a shot.

We chatted. He was charming. I found it easy to relate to him as a person, not just as a visitor who had to be entertained as part of the job. Time passed very quickly.

He looked at his watch. "I have to go on somewhere else. Would you like to go for something to eat after you finish work?"

"Yes, sure," I said (as if I wouldn't!). "But I don't finish here until three o'clock. . . ."

"Doesn't matter," he said easily. "I'll be back for you at three."

As I left the Kokusai, he called to me from a brand-new BMW sports car. He smiled as he held open the door. "What sort of food do you eat?"

"Oh, whatever you like," I said, sinking back into the luxury of the upholstered seat. He took me to a Chinese restaurant, not one that catered to the tourists, but an authentic Chinese establishment. I'd been to such places, but only with Chinese companions, as there were no English-speaking waiters. They certainly had the best food.

The meal was wonderful, and James was attentive and talkative.

"What do you do for a living?" I asked, as the waiters brought yet another interesting delicacy to the table.

"Oh, cars, mostly." He speared a fragment of meat with a chopstick. "I own a showroom—BMW's. I'm in exports and imports."

"Sounds very interesting." I probed further. "You said 'mostly.' What else do you do?"

"I follow motor racing," he replied. "I go to the big meetings whenever I can manage it. Sometimes in Europe."

I liked the fact that he enjoyed travel. Most of the men I had gotten to know in Hong Kong rarely traveled beyond it, and I didn't often find someone who understood my own wanderlust. We talked about my journey to Hong Kong, and he prompted me with occasional questions, the sort you can only ask if you know the places yourself. He said very little about himself, but was interested in my family, my home in England, and my plans after Hong Kong. By the time the meal was over, he had learned quite a lot about me.

He drove me back to my apartment. He asked for my telephone number, and when I gave it to him, asked if he could see me the next night. I agreed.

I let myself in, flopped onto the bed, and kicked my shoes off. Sue popped her head around the door. "Good time, was it?"

I gazed at her. "Sue," I announced raptly, "I think I'm going to like James."

We were soon meeting regularly. I'd met many men in Hong Kong, but James was different. He had all the glamour I wanted—he was rich, foreign, and had a hint of mystery about him. I felt safe with him. I didn't consider money to be very important in my life, but having tasted the pleasures of wealth, I found I enjoyed them. He was considerate and generous; he often gave me presents, and he always had enough money to go where we wanted and do what we wanted.

From the first, I thought James was very sweet. He sometimes seemed surprisingly young for his age, though at other times he looked old and hard. At the beginning of our relationship I found myself wanting to mother him, and that was always a part of my feelings for him. But he was affectionate too; he would kiss me without warning, when I was least expecting it. I loved his shyness. He was reserved in public, but when we were alone we would cuddle in each other's arms for hours. I even enjoyed his fits of jealousy. He once forbade me to go out with another man who'd taken me to lunch, and was adamant about it.

He was always interested in my family, and often asked about my mother. Sometimes he would give me money and say, "Why don't you ring your mother?" My family was very important to me, and that was something else I could share with James. And on top of all his good qualities, he was stunningly good-looking! Gradually I was falling in love. Sooner or later, I knew, we would end up in bed. I didn't mind; I wanted to. Perhaps, I told myself, this was really it, what I had been looking for.

We spent hours driving around Hong Kong at night. James adored fast cars, was a very fast driver, and was also a very good one. He'd pick me up from the club at three o'clock and we'd go off, anywhere. Though Hong Kong City has the distinction of being the most densely populated city on earth, the countryside in the north of the Colony is sparsely populated. At three in the morning the country roads are virtually empty, and Hong Kong has some very fast roads. I think we were as close to each other then as we ever were, just sharing each other's company, hurtling through Hong Kong in the sleepy hours before dawn.

In my job I'd become skillful at persuading men to talk about themselves, but James preserved his air of mystery. I knew he had been living in Amsterdam, but when I asked him where he was living in Hong Kong, he didn't answer directly. "Oh, . . . nearby. I'm waiting to get my own place now that I'm back from Europe. I'm living with my aunt and uncle. They're old-style Chinese—I couldn't take a girl back there. And there isn't much point in giving you the phone number. They don't speak English."

He rarely went into the Kokusai, though he was usually waiting for me when I left work. I never needed to telephone him anyway; he was always there, and I spent most of my free time with him. Sometimes he would suddenly announce that he had to go to Taiwan or somewhere else for a few days, but he always rang me as soon as he got back, and he brought me beautiful presents.

One day quite early in our relationship I got a message from James asking me to meet him at a restaurant we'd been to occasionally—a bistro where a Filipino played guitar. James greeted me at the door. "I want you to meet a friend of mine," he said and took me over to meet Simon Lo.

A youngish man in his thirties rose politely to shake hands. I tried not to stare at the enormous scar running from his forehead to his jawline. Whatever had caused it must have just missed his left eye.

Despite the scar (maybe because of it) he was very good-looking, and he had a broad smile.

James ordered our meal. After a few pleasantries he smiled apologetically at me. "Excuse me," he said and began a lengthy conversation with Simon in Chinese. It was quite usual for this to happen when we were with James's Chinese friends, and there was nothing out of the ordinary in it. One of James's good points as far as I was concerned was the fact that he always apologized to me courteously before starting a foreign conversation—most of the other Chinese men I knew tended simply to turn their backs on me and get on with it.

Simon seemed to be around quite often, and there were frequent long Chinese conversations, during which I enjoyed my meal or gazed around whatever glamorous nightspot we happened to be in. James was always especially attentive to me afterward. Once, half-exasperated, I teased him. "Do you have to bring him with you every time? Is he your body-guard or something?" We both laughed.

We spent one of my days off in Macao, the old Portuguese territory near Hong Kong. Macao moves at a slower pace than Hong Kong, and it was a relief for me to get away from the ceaseless bustle and wander around the ancient buildings and monu-ments, painlessly absorbing centuries of Portuguese history.

We ended up in one of the city's numerous casinos. James was an expert gambler, and rich enough to indulge his taste. We wedged ourselves into a crowd of people standing around the gaming table, and I screamed with delight as James began a winning streak.

"You're bringing me luck," he grinned. He shoved a pile of chips into my hands. "Here. Now you try for a while."

He had to show me how to bet, but I was soon flipping the chips onto the table like an expert, biting my fingernails as the wheel rattled around. I jumped up and down and clasped James's arm as the croupier pushed a stack of chips over to me. Some of the other players laughed and applauded. James smiled.

"See? You are lucky. Now, . . . we'll try our luck at blackjack."

The evening was wonderful. I lost count of whether we were winning or losing. James told me that the chips he had given me had been hundred-dollar chips. It was staggering; I'd been throwing them down like confetti. Eventually, we left the casino and made our way back to the ferry. At Hong Kong, we drove to the Peninsular Hotel at the end of Nathan Road. Anybody living in Hong Kong knows about the Peninsular Hotel. It's one of the oldest in the Colony, dating from the days when it was the hotel rail passengers used while awaiting the train to Europe. It's still an exclusive and very expensive place, and I'd often seen the fleet of Rolls Royces provided for the use of guests.

The evening was turning into a fairytale. "Fantastic!" I exclaimed, when James announced calmly, "We'll stay here tonight." He'd booked an enormous suite with all the trimmings. I couldn't believe it was happening.

We became lovers that night. It was wonderful and it was inevitable. Part of me still wanted to hold back. I'd had a string of relationships which had left me unsatisfied. What could make me think James could give me what I wanted? I was suddenly aware of all the differences between us.

"Don't be silly; don't get too involved here," one part of me was saying. But another part of me argued back: "Well, you're having a good time, he's nice to you, he doesn't push you into anything; so why pull out now?" We became closer and closer.

We'd been seeing each other for about three months when he came to me with some news.

"I'm going to Europe on business, Rita."

I was disappointed. "Oh, James, do you have to?"

"I'm afraid so. I can't change my plans. It's really important."

"When will you be back?"

He didn't answer the question, but asked me one instead. "Don't you have some holiday due to you?"

My eyes sparkled as I began to see what he was leading up to. "Yes—a fortnight."

"Well, I've a plan that will mean you can see your mother and family for a while."

I gasped. "James! How. . . ."

"Simple. You come with me as far as Paris; then we split up. I look after my business deals, and you go on to England and see your mother. I'll pay all your expenses to Blackburn and back."

I was still badly bitten by the travel bug, and I was missing my mother very much. I knew it wasn't the right time to go back to England for good, but here was James offering me an all-expenses paid trip to Blackburn, with the return ticket in my pocket as an effective reply to any pressure that might be put on me to stay. I agreed joyfully. I did want to see Mother again.

We planned the trip. James had far-reaching plans beyond my return from Blackburn. I'd evaded conversations previously about where our relationship was heading; now James was very direct.

"When we get back, we'll get an apartment together. Wouldn't you like that?"

I wasn't sure.

"Well, then; we'll get married if you'd rather do that. What do you think?"

It was all happening too quickly for me. I guess I was scared. I told him I didn't think I was ready for marriage. "But an apartment is a nice idea. We could do that." It didn't commit me, it kept my options open, and I enjoyed his company anyway.

If anybody had told me twelve months before that within a year I would be a hostess in a glamorous nightclub in Hong Kong, rubbing shoulders with the rich and famous, I wouldn't have believed him. Yet here I was, with a rich boyfriend, a nice place to live, friendly workmates, and a lifestyle which included fast cars, expensive restaurants, yachts, and film stars, calmly discussing a joyride halfway across the Western world. It was what I'd always wanted; it was what my traveling had been for.

And yet . . . and yet. Despite everything, I was miserable. A young girl in a foreign city can find herself desperately lonely, even when surrounded by people; and though loneliness was only part of my depression, it was a focus I could concentrate on. I needed James. He was attentive, and he genuinely seemed to care for me as a person. However I rationalized it, he was someone to cling to. And I did.

Even my love for James couldn't dispel my unhappiness completely. I dreaded going home and being on my own. I knew there was something desperately wrong, and I didn't know what it was. I used to get home sometimes, put one of my favorite Rod Stewart records on the record player, fling myself onto my bed, and cry and cry. I used to rage at myself: "Well, what do you want? Is it marriage you're after?" I would demand. "Do you want to go back to Australia, marry the good man you left behind? Is that what you want? No, you just came from there. You couldn't settle down. Do you want to live at home? Are you missing your mother? You know very well that you tried that for twelve months and it just drove you both crazy—you ended up even falling out with her. You couldn't settle down there either. . . . So what do you want? You've got what you've always set your heart on. You've got this glamorous life, this amazing boyfriend. You've got everything you ever wanted, haven't you?"

I had no answers to my questions. I didn't know what I wanted. I didn't even know the right questions to ask.

5 Arrest

*I haven't been able to write much
before now . . . it's an odd feeling
wanting to wake up from a nightmare
and eventually realizing it's no dream.*

Letter to Mother, April 19, 1977

I looked forward to my trip to Europe with great
excitement. I thought about writing home to say I
was coming, but decided against it. It would be so
good to surprise Mother, simply to knock on her
door, and see her face when she saw me standing
there. I couldn't resist giving her just a hint on the
telephone. We'd planned for her to come to Hong
Kong later in the year, and while calling her one
day, I casually mentioned that she might possibly

see me before then. She hadn't the faintest idea what I was talking about.

I kept on working. James wouldn't commit himself to a date for our departure, so I carried on as usual, working at the Kokusai and seeing him at night. Finally one night I left the club and saw him standing by his car holding two tickets. It was settled; we would leave on March 17.

"Make sure you are packed and ready in the morning. I'll pick you up at your apartment," he said.

March 17, I suddenly realized, was St. Patrick's Day—the day on which, several years before, I had first left England for Australia.

I began to worry about luggage. I'd come a long way since arriving in Hong Kong with my ancient knapsack, but that was still the only luggage I possessed. I didn't fancy cramming my things into it for a trip to Europe. When I mentioned this, James presented me with three expensive suitcases of his own, in hand-stitched soft leather. He pointed out that I would need warm clothes if I was going to England in March. He took out his wallet and handed over two hundred dollars for a new wardrobe. He shrugged aside my thanks. I had a great time spending the money.

I got everything packed and sat in my apartment on the morning of the great day. When the doorbell chimed, I rushed to let James in. One look at his face told me immediately that something had gone wrong.

"What's happened?"

"I really am sorry, Rita. Something's come up. I will have to stay here for the next few days on business. I can't possibly come with you today."

I stared at him, dismayed. "Well, I'm not going if you're not. Let's forget it."

He shook his head. "That's not possible. The tickets are paid for, and it's too late to cancel."

"You can afford to lose the money."

"That's not the point. It's stupid for you not to go. You've been looking forward to it."

"How could I possibly go now?"

James outlined his alternative plan. "Look, Rita. You can fly via Bangkok. You leave here today, get to Bangkok tomorrow, stop over there, and fly on to Europe. We meet up in Paris. So we only have to alter the first bit of the plan."

"Is it worth the trouble?" I didn't like this change of plan.

"Worth it? Of course it is. You get an extra holiday in Bangkok. Arrive in Paris with a nice tan. I'll pay the extra. Don't worry."

I hesitated. I didn't want to appear ungrateful, but I didn't want to go on my own, not after looking forward to going away with James. I tried to explain this to him. He produced his trump card. By coincidence, Simon Lo was traveling to Bangkok that day. He would fly on the same flight as mine, book in at the same hotel, and handle all the bills. "You'll have no problems," James assured me. "Simon will look after you."

The change of plan left me a little uneasy. Odd ideas flitted through my mind. Was James getting bored with me? Was this some complicated method of ditching me? I decided that couldn't be right. It was too complicated a way of going about it. In the end I agreed to the new suggestion, though I wasn't too happy about Simon suddenly appearing in the plan. On the other hand, James's travel arrangements were often haphazard, and he would change his plans at the last minute. The last thing in my mind was the possibility that this change of plan might have any sinister purpose.

Was I so stupid to think that I could have a holiday with a handsome, rich, young boyfriend—for nothing? I didn't think so for one minute. Scores of men had asked me to go on similar trips at the Kokusai, but I'd always said no because I'd never cared for the men. James was different. He was my lover, not some boring old middle-aged charmer who'd walked into the Kokusai.

Simon met me at Kai Tak Airport for the Bangkok flight. I hadn't often been on my own with him. He was pleasant enough, but rather distant. He handed me a new radio cassette player. "From James—a present for your mother."

We said little on the flight; Simon buried his head in a newspaper, and I had my own thoughts.

It was lovely to be back in Bangkok. We checked into the Asia Hotel, taking separate rooms, and had dinner together that evening. Simon was punctilious and courteous, but conversation was intermittent. I hardly saw him after that first evening. I had some shopping to do the next day; James had given me some spending money. I spent some of the day lazing by the hotel pool and the rest of it sightseeing.

Under the present monarch, King Bhumibol Adulyadej, Thailand's westernization has advanced dramatically, but it's still a land of contrasts. I wandered around modern department stores and ancient temples, down streets where Western dress and traditional Thai silks appeared side by side. The heat was welcome after Hong Kong, which had been quite cool when we left. Down by the river, tourists thronged the tree-lined boulevards. I bought my lunch from a street trader's stall and ate it in a shady corner of a public square where businessmen sat among saffron-robed monks.

The Paris flight was scheduled for 11:00 P.M. the next day. I had to check out of my hotel room by noon. Simon, who was staying on, suggested that I leave my things in his room, and helped me to move them. He suggested I take advantage of the Asia Hotel's beauty salon, and I booked an appointment for four o'clock. I whiled away the time sightseeing and shopping, then went back to Simon's room to get some money from my luggage.

Simon didn't answer my knock immediately. When he appeared, he held the door closed behind him. He sounded embarrassed. I assumed that he had found himself a woman. I explained what I wanted, and he went back into the room, closing the door, and reappeared with a bundle of money—500 *baht,* which I wasn't going to refuse. So I didn't go into his room, and I hadn't seen my luggage since noon.

The beauty salon was fantastic. Simon, I discovered, had paid in advance, probably to be free of me for the afternoon. I had a steam bath, massage, facial, manicure, pedicure, and shampoo and set—all for the equivalent of ten English pounds (approximately $18 in U.S. currency). At seven o'clock we had dinner together and drinks afterward in the hotel bar. Then I went to his room to use his shower. My luggage was there, waiting for me. I took a few odds and ends out for the journey. Most of the clothes in the bags were winter ones, and it was about ninety degrees in Bangkok.

At about 9:30, Simon came down to the foyer with me and called a taxi to take me to the airport. When the taxi arrived, he kissed me on the cheek. It was the closest we'd been for the whole trip. He smiled at me coolly. "Take good care of yourself!" He waved and went back into the hotel.

Soon I was at the airport.

Then the nightmare began.

6 Detained

I think I'm going to need more than a good lawyer. . . .

Letter to Aunt Margaret and Tom,
June 10, 1977

"Who are you?"

The icy words reverberated in my head. I stared in disbelief.

Simon turned away from me with a sneer and reached for his trousers. Sobbing and shouting, I leaped at him, my fists whirling. The police seized me. The captain pointed to the door. "Take her outside to wait."

I argued hysterically with the policewoman, in the front seat of the police car. They brought Simon down after a few minutes and bundled him into the back seat with a policeman. He looked disheveled, as if he had thrown his clothes onto his body. As we drove off, I subsided into exhausted silence. Simon sat calmly behind me, saying nothing. I didn't look out of the window and had no idea where we were going.

The cars pulled up in the courtyard of a large brick building, several stories high. It was still dark. The policewoman helped me out, and we went inside. It was some sort of police station. She exchanged a few words with the police captain and took me upstairs. On the bare landing she took a key from her pocket and opened the door of a cell. I shrank back in horror. The cell was dark and dirty, and several large cockroaches scuttled across the floor. I've always been terrified of cockroaches, even small ones. These were large, glossy brutes, like ones I'd seen—and avoided—in Australia.

"I can't go in there. I can't go in," I pleaded with the policewoman. She shook her head and smiled sympathetically.

"You'll feel better in the morning," she said. She gently pushed me forward and locked the door firmly behind me.

I was standing in a small room, one wall of which was a floor-to-ceiling grille of bars with the door in it. Most of the space was occupied by a raised wooden platform which I took to be my bed. Through a doorless doorway I could see the back of the cell, where a trough and a water pipe were visible. A tin dipper lay in a puddle of water in the trough. Nearby was the toilet: two wooden footrests, with a hole in the floor between them. Somebody had provided a piece of dirty hardboard to cover the doorway and secure some privacy. It was only waist high, and had slipped over on the sloppy floor.

The dipper-shower and the simple toilet weren't new to me. I'd seen them in Bali; they're very common in the Far East. But it was very different seeing them in the spacious, airy rooms of Bali hostels and friends' houses. There they had been fun, part of the exotic pleasures of travel, a symbol of the passion most Far Eastern people have for cleanliness. In the dark cell they just looked squalid, and had been left none too clean by previous inhabitants.

I wandered around the little cell, my mind in confusion. The policewoman reappeared with a bundle of my clothes. "We must keep your bags for now," she explained. I accepted the bundle gratefully. Picking out a few pullovers and skirts, I constructed a makeshift bed on the wooden pallet and lay down. It was harder than any bed I'd slept on for a long time. Outside the cell door, an electric light had been left on. I pulled the clothes over my head and tried to sleep. Time passed, but I lost track of it.

A movement outside made me look up. A skinny, very short man in vest and pants was looking in at me. I was suddenly aware of a raging thirst. Seeing him, I croaked, "Drink! Drink!"

He grinned and extended cupped hands. "Money!"

I'd changed my money at the airport, and had only French francs. I offered him a banknote. He waved his hand dismissively. He pointed at my bracelet. "Nice. I take it. Give you water."

I turned my face to the wall and wept in frustration. I didn't understand the way things operated in prison, and this trading for water seemed barbaric and cruel. I screamed at my tormenter, "Dog! Dog!" He only chuckled. When I looked around again, he had disappeared.

More time passed. There was a jangle of keys. I sat up. The police captain was opening the cell door; he came in, locking it behind him. He looked as if he had had a good sleep.

My clothes were sticking to me in the heat, and my face was hot and sticky. He looked at me sympathetically. "Are you thirsty?"

I nodded. "A man came—he wouldn't take my money—he wouldn't give me water. . . ."

"Ah! The catman. He feeds the cats, you see. It is to keep the vermin down."

I shuddered. The captain called to somebody outside the cell, and there was a clatter of feet down the stairs. "He is getting you a Coke," he explained.

"But I haven't any *baht.* . . ."

"Don't worry. It doesn't matter."

The Coke arrived in the usual polyethylene bag, tied at one end with a straw sticking out. It was warm but very welcome. I drank it gratefully. There was food as well—some kind of rice dish. I couldn't face it. It was days before I managed to bring myself to eat again.

The captain was a frequent visitor to my cell.

"How long are you going to keep me here?" I demanded.

The captain waved a hand genially. "Oh, . . . maybe six days, maybe thirty. . . ." Without waiting for a reply, he began to ask me questions.

"What do you know about Alan Soon?"

I had never heard the name, and said so. But he kept returning to the same question.

"How did you meet Alan Soon? When did you arrange to fly with him?"

"I don't know anybody called Alan Soon. . . ."

"What was your rendezvous plan with him?"

"I don't know what you're talking about. . . . Who is this Alan Soon guy, anyway?"

Eventually the captain told me. "Soon was flying with you. He was in the Customs Hall when you were arrested. Come, Miss Nightingale, you must have seen him."

I suddenly remembered the flint-eyed Chinese man who had been watching while my bags were searched.

"Tell me the whole story, one more time," said the captain, flipping the pages of his notebook.

I told my story repeatedly, hoping desperately that I was telling it the same each time, because my head got so confused about the chain of events. I became very despondent. The captain comforted me.

"Don't worry. Those other two, Soon and Lo; we know they're involved in drugs. They're well known to the police. We've been watching them for a long time. But you're not being held on a drugs charge. We're holding you under Article 21. That's breach of the peace. Your lawyer will explain everything."

"My lawyer?"

"Of course! You will have a lawyer. Your Embassy will arrange it."

"I must let James know. He's meeting me in Paris."

The captain gave me an odd look. "The British Embassy will arrange all that."

As he was leaving, I said, "How long will I be in here? When will you let me out?"

He paused at the door. "We have to hold you here for thirty days. It is the law. You'll be all right. You'll see." He scratched his nose. "How much money do you have?"

I didn't want to seem rich and therefore a possible drug smuggler, so I said that I had a few dollars in Australia. Later I met people who had bribed their way out of trouble, and wondered what would have happened if I had tried to do so then. The captain merely nodded, said, "Don't worry," and went downstairs.

I was fingerprinted several times and photographed holding a placard with an identity number and an inscription in Thai. Dozens of people—officials, other detainees and others—came to the cell to look at me. Once I woke up and saw a guard watching me. He was leaning against the wall outside, looking unbearably cool and relaxed in his official uniform of khaki drill trousers and shirt. I scowled at him.

"What d'you think you're staring at?" I demanded.

He offered a pack of cigarettes. "Would you like one?"

"No, I wouldn't."

He lit a cigarette and inhaled thoughtfully. "You know, I'm really very sorry about what's happened. I'm really very sorry indeed. . . ."

He was trying to cheer me up, but I was in no mood to be consoled. After a while he went away.

I wondered when I would hear from the Embassy and when a lawyer would arrive. I began to fret about my mother. What would she say when they heard about all this? I imagined her opening an official letter and reading a formal announcement that her daughter had been detained in connection with heroin smuggling. What would her reaction be? Would she know whom to contact, what to do? I brooded over the grief that this was going to cause my family, and I couldn't bear the thought. I even imagined her deserted by her friends and neighbors because of the disgrace that I had brought upon Blackburn. I didn't know then that the people of Blackburn would support my mother the way that they did. I thought I would be condemned, and that Mother would suffer.

In fact she learned the story in the worst possible way. On the day following my arrest, an item appeared in the newspapers. A Reuter's correspondent in Bangkok had cabled the story to England, and my sister Ann saw it in that night's *Lancashire Evening Telegraph*. Mother had just that brief paragraph to go on until more detailed news arrived from the Embassy. It was weeks before I could bring myself to write. If I was going to be out after thirty days, I thought, it would be better not to write for a month than have Mother get a letter from me on police notepaper.

I was taken to an office for yet another interview. This time it was my lawyer. He was a Thai gentleman, with a round, pleasant face. Despite the heat, he wore a dark suit and tie and carried a small briefcase, which he placed carefully on the desk. He shook hands soberly.

"My name is Sorochai," he announced. "My firm is Tilleke and Gibbins. It is a very long established law company in Bangkok. The British Embassy has asked us to help you." He took a neatly folded handkerchief from his pocket and carefully mopped his brow. "I am very sorry that you are in trouble."

Opening his briefcase, he transferred a bundle of papers onto the desk. "I must ask you what happened. Please tell me the whole story."

He listened patiently, his hands placed together, pursing his lips and nodding. Occasionally he asked me to repeat a part of the story. "I see, I see," he murmured. "Go on."

I finished. Mr. Sorochai was sitting back in his chair, looking at the ceiling, deep in thought. I could hear people shouting in the courtyard outside. He slowly lowered his gaze until he was looking at me. He sighed.

"Well?" I demanded rudely. Mr. Sorochai raised his eyebrows. My voice tightened. "What's going to happen? When can I leave?"

He looked at me appraisingly. "I think this is a very difficult case," he said flatly.

"But it wasn't my heroin. I knew nothing about it; they *must* release me!"

"This is difficult," he intoned. He gathered his papers together and placed them carefully into his briefcase. Standing up, he extended his hand. "I will be back very soon," he promised. "There is much to do. Papers must be obtained; questions must be asked. The courts here do not move quickly. It is for your protection."

At the door he bowed gravely as I was led back to my cell. "I am sorry. This is not an easy case. Be patient."

The next day I was taken to another large room in

the building. It was like a small courtroom. On one side were a number of benches, and on the other a long table. Behind the table a number of people were seated. An English woman was, I found later, the British Consul. Two or three official-looking people sat in the center, flanked by military officers in full braid and insignia. I sat on one of the benches. A policewoman sat next to me.

Two more police officers arrived, escorting two men. When I saw who they were, my heart raced. They were Simon Lo and Alan Soon.

I was being prodded to stand up. The man who appeared to be in charge was an Englishman.

"You are Rita Nightingale?" His voice was level, his manner efficient and as crisp as his uniform. I nodded. The policewoman nudged me. "Yes," I said faintly.

"I am an Interpol officer. Do you understand what Interpol is?"

"Yes."

"Your home is in Australia? Your nationality is British? On what date did you leave Australia?"

The questions followed each other like machine-gun fire. I answered mechanically. I was questioned about my job in Hong Kong, about the trip to Paris, and about James. They wanted dates, times, all sorts of details. I told them all I could remember. Before long I was permitted to sit down. It was Lo's and Soon's turn to be questioned. Their interrogation seemed to be the real reason for the interview. They refused to answer questions, looking straight ahead. The Englishman tried to make them respond; then the other officials interrogated them in various Asian dialects. They remained silent and tight-lipped. The meeting ended abruptly. The officials left the room and we were taken away. Neither Lo nor Soon acknowledged me in any way.

No word came from James. I was worried that my arrest had caused problems for him. He was planning to meet me in Paris, and I wasn't going to be there— he would be frantic with worry. I'd given James's name and the address of the hotel we were to meet at, to the police at the airport.

A niggling fear began to grow at the back of my mind. People asked me questions about James, but when I asked them if any word had come from him, they were noncommittal. Other prisoners in the police station said I was a fool to have been involved with him. I began to remember the questions about him that the Interpol team had asked.

Worry for James was soon replaced by anger. Whatever had gone wrong with the arrangements, he could at least have gotten in touch with me. I decided I was going to have some strong things to say to James Wong when I got back to Hong Kong.

I lapsed into a sullen bitterness. I was furious that nobody was prepared to see that the whole thing was a misunderstanding. Instead, I was going to have to hang around in a cell for a month while the thing got sorted out. James was having a good time in Paris and I was stuck in Bangkok. I didn't even know the procedure for getting released. I hoped that somebody would come and explain to me how the Thai legal system worked, but nobody did. I pieced together what I could from odd comments people made, but I was confused about it all.

The captain who was responsible for me was very

friendly. After the first flurry of interviews was over and things had begun to settle down into a dull routine, he sent for me. I was taken upstairs to the large general office, a large room with a pair of ancient filing cabinets and a number of desks. The captain looked up and smiled as I came in.

"Rita, you look pale. You need some fresh air!" He waved me over to his desk, which was near an open window. Papers lifted and rustled in a gentle breeze. I sat down. Two enormous fans in the ceiling creaked rhythmically overhead. I looked outside. In the courtyard was one of the food stalls that are found everywhere in Bangkok. A bored teenage stall keeper lounged in its shadow. People were talking to each other in shaded corners; uniformed officials were going about their business; I could hear the cheerful noises of traffic. It all looked beautifully normal. I swallowed, suddenly aware of a lump in my throat. The captain rubbed his hands together noisily.

"Hah! You have not been eating," he scolded me. "You must eat, you know. Pretty girl like you must not starve! You're not on a diet, I hope?"

I smiled wanly and shook my head.

"Right!" he said enthusiastically. "What do you want to eat?"

"I don't know what there is."

"Well, do you like fried rice? Noodles? Noodles are very nice."

I decided I was quite hungry. He sent one of the office boys to get the food, and I watched the boy appear below me in the courtyard and consult with the stall keeper. As he walked back carefully carrying a bowl of food, I envied him the simple freedom to go where he wanted.

I perched on the captain's desk, eating noodles and drinking Coca-Cola. We talked and talked about anything and everything—travel, films we'd seen, things in the news. I responded to him because he had sat down and listened to my version of what had happened, but I liked him anyway; he was good-humored and sympathetic. It was only when I raised the matter of my release that he became vague and evasive.

When the captain sent for somebody to take me back to my cell, I was calmer and almost cheerful. During my detention at the police station he sent for me several times and allowed me to sit at his desk.

The return of Mr. Sorochai brought hardly any encouragement; there was no definite news. He came several times, bringing a gift of food or drink with him, and a supply of magazines—after I begged him for something to read. He dressed immaculately; though he always looked hot in his suit, he declined invitations to take his jacket off. He was friendly and usually had time to chat. He mentioned once that his wife was expecting their first baby, and we told each other about our families.

He didn't smile very often. I wanted him to and tried to break his reserve with jokes, but he maintained a somber expression. I wanted him to smile because it would have made matters seem less ominous. Though he never scowled, and was gentle and courteous, his refusal to make light of my problems made me increasingly worried. His repeated assurances that much work was being done on my case made me no less alarmed. He was definite about one thing. There was to be no overnight miracle. I was going to have to spend the full thirty days in the police station.

"And then?" I persisted.

But Mr. Sorochai would not make any reply to that.

When I walked out of that cell back into the outside world, I vowed, it was going to be with head held high and eyes bright. One thing was for sure; I wasn't going to vegetate. I began looking for things with which to occupy myself.

I persuaded the guards to give me cleaning materials and started to clean the cell. I had a rag which I used to scrub the floor. Then I started on the crevices in the wood and the grimy bars of the cell.

As my frustration increased, my temper grew shorter. I snapped at everybody and complained bitterly about everything. I was a far from well-behaved prisoner. Once I was doing something which involved the use of a small pair of manicure scissors. A sudden exclamation outside the cell made me look up. A guard was pointing at the scissors and holding out his hand for them. Thinking he wanted to trim his fingernails, I passed them out to him, whereupon he immediately put them into his pocket.

"Why did you do that?" I demanded fiercely.

"Not allowed!" stated the guard matter of factly. "Weapon. Sharp!"

I lost my temper and shouted at him, swearing like a trooper. "What do you mean, you stupid idiot?" I howled. I pointed to a row of bottles standing in the cell, which had held sauce and cold drinks. I waved one of them at him. "What do you think this is? Isn't this a weapon?"

I stood there shaking, holding the bottle. I wanted to smash it on the bars to prove my point. The guard, looking at me as if I were mad, laughed, and walked away.

The Foreign Office in London issued a somber statement to the effect that court action might well turn out to be a lengthy business. For the present, they intended to watch carefully and keep a low profile. "She is legally represented, but there is nothing new. We have advised her relatives this could take some time. We don't know how long."

I was never quite sure what precisely was happening about my case, as life at the police station ground slowly on. None of the officials were unkind to me. In fact the general attitude shown to me was one of offhandedness, of submitting to tedious routines. Various Embassy staff were sympathetic and concerned, but were not able to give me any more information or say how things would turn out. I was grateful to the Vice-Consul—amazingly, he was a Blackburn man—who, as he left the interview room with his colleagues, turned back to me, smiled encouragingly, and said, "Keep your chin up, lass!"

Food was being sent to me in my cell. Even at first, when I could not face the idea of food and made no arrangements to buy any, meals appeared— good ones at that. I assumed it was the normal police station food, but eventually I gathered that standard prison food was very plain and simple. When a Thai girl was put in the cell with me later, we shared all sorts of delicacies brought in by her family, including a bottle of brandy. Obviously this wasn't prison fare; I began to wonder again what the system was and where my own luxurious food was coming from.

Sitting in the captain's office one day, I was looking down at the food stall. I suddenly asked him, "The food that comes to my cell—is that provided by the government?"

The captain grinned broadly. "The government? No! They provide good food, but not like what you are eating. That's from your friend downstairs."

"What do you mean?"

"You know—your friend, Simon Lo. He's in a cell downstairs. He buys the food for you."

"He's not my friend! I won't eat it!" I screamed, and for a few days I did refuse it, though later I accepted it again, thinking I may as well use Simon seeing that he had used me. When eventually I left the police station, Simon and Alan Soon were still being held. I know, because I was asked, "Do you want to say good-bye to your friends?"

"They're not my friends!" I shouted again. A week afterward, they were deported from Thailand.

One Thursday, when I had been in detention for twenty-six days, Mr. Sorochai arrived with news.

"Next week the thirty days are up. You will be going to court." He arranged where he would meet me at the courthouse and various other details.

The following morning I woke up in confusion. Somebody was shaking my shoulders.

"Huh? What—what time is it?"

The policewoman released my shoulders. "It's six

o'clock. You must get up. This morning you go to court."

"Today? That's crazy! I'm not supposed to go till next week!"

She was unperturbed. "Please dress. You must be ready quickly. And pack your belongings. You must bring them with you."

As I gathered my things, I argued frantically. "Look, are you sure you got it right?" I groped for my jeans and slipped into them. "My lawyer doesn't know. How can I go to court if my lawyer isn't here? Why am I going, anyway? What's going to happen?" I began to throw clothes and other possessions into my bags. "I want my lawyer. Please, will somebody call Mr. Sorochai?"

I was driven in a Landrover through the city, demanding, "What's happening? Why are we going today? Where's my lawyer? Why hasn't my lawyer been told?"

"You won't need your lawyer," the officials replied.

7 Lard Yao

*I know you are strong, Mother, and
believe me, I am going to be the
same. It is no good for me now to
look back and say, I should have had
more sense or I should have had an
idea. I cannot go back, only forward.
. . .Don't be upset too much, Mother,
I have done the crying for both of us.*

Letter to Mother, April 19, 1977

The courthouse was a large building of grubby
stone with an imposing flight of steps. At the back
was a courtyard. A senior officer told me to sit there
and then disappeared into the building. People
thronged the yard, and the usual food booths were
everywhere. In the distance I could hear traffic

noises, people laughing and shouting to each other outside the courtyard.

I suddenly realized that I was alone and unguarded. I could have got up and walked away. Numbly, I contemplated how it might possibly work. I knew a well-known hotel in Bangkok where I had stayed, where friends of mine had been able to get fake passports and documents. There was a Frenchman there who had the whole thing organized. And after that? Well, I had friends all over the East. . . .

But I was too confused and frightened to get up and walk away. And I was still thinking, *It can't be all that serious. I'm not involved, after all. It wasn't my heroin. I must be all right. After all, I'm only being held under Article 21.*

I was frightened, though. Sitting in the courtyard, I asked each passerby, "Do you speak English?" Eventually somebody sent a Thai woman lawyer over to me—Jennifer, who spoke excellent English. I explained that my lawyer didn't know I'd come to court.

"Oh, that will be all right. I'll give him a telephone call." He had given me his telephone number; I gave it to Jennifer.

"They shot a guy this morning, you know."

I looked at her incredulously.

"Yes, he was a Chinese guy on drug charges. The American drug enforcement officers are over here at the moment." She grinned. "Don't worry. I'll see your lawyer is told you are here."

My officer returned and motioned me to pick up my bags. Now in greater fear than ever, I was led into a huge courtroom. Some Thai prisoners were already there, seated on the floor. The men were in leg irons, and there were a few women prisoners. Many of them were handcuffed together. The guard brought a chair for me; I was the only prisoner to be given one. As I sat down, he leaned toward me and murmured, "You know, I feel so sorry for you."

The black-gowned judges entered. One began to read names from a long list. I assumed that they were names, because people were standing up and sitting down as the list was read. The proceedings were in Thai. Suddenly the guard poked me in the ribs. I had missed my name. I stood up. A moment later he tugged my arm and I sat down again.

"What's going on?" I whispered.

"Oh, prison," he said. "You're going to prison."

I burst into tears. "Where is my lawyer?" I wept. "I want to see him. I want my lawyer." The guard repeated, "I feel sorry for you, I feel sorry for you."

At the back of the court my bags were unceremoniously emptied into a large cardboard box, which was handed to me. I was taken to a cell in the courthouse. It was about twenty-five feet across. At least eighty Thai women were in there. The noise was indescribable. Some were eating; others were holding shouted conversations above the general uproar.

A guard began to examine the contents of my box systematically, presumably looking for dangerous weapons. She removed a razor, a pair of tweezers, some aspirin, and other items and put them on one side. As the lovely clothes I had bought for Paris were taken from the box one by one, the women fell upon them with cries of delight. Horrified, I watched the clothes pass from hand to hand and disappear from view. The guard appeared oblivious.

I didn't know where I was; I was in a trance. I thought I was in prison already. I'd no idea what the inside of a prison would be like, but this was bad enough to fulfill my worst expectations. I stood helpless at the edge of the cell, looking at the mass of women. Gradually I realized that some of them were gesturing to me. When I didn't respond, they pulled me by the sleeves, across the room. I picked my way past seated and prone figures. I was being dragged to the far wall, where through a six-foot gap scores of people outside were gesticulating to the prisoners, shouting to them above the din, trying to establish contact. As I neared the gap, I saw a familiar Thai face. It was Mr. Sorochai.

"What's happening?" I shouted desperately. "I can't stand it. I don't know what's happening. You've got to get me out of here!"

He smiled, a rare thing for him. "Don't worry," he called. "We are applying for bail. Just wait a little longer." In the press of people he was flustered and hot, but he beamed confidently. "Don't worry!"

"You must get me out now," I insisted. "I'll go mad—I can't stay here. I can't!"

As I was pushed back by the crowd into the clamorous room, he called after me, "Don't worry. It will be all right, you'll see. . . ."

All my possessions found their way back to me, after the other occupants of the cell had satisfied their curiosity. The Thai people are insatiably inquisitive about anything European. I was confused and resentful, and snatched my things back angrily as they came within reach.

I heard the other prisoners talking about me. *"Farang. . . . Aayuu towrai? . . . Geh. . . ."* ("A foreigner. . . . How old? . . . A young one. . . .") An English-speaking Thai girl was offering me food, but I refused. I sat and brooded. It was still like a bad dream. Half an hour later my name was called. I was taken to a police office in the building. As I was brought in, a dapper figure rose to his feet. It was Mr. Sorochai. "Don't worry," he said and sat down heavily. "We are applying for bail."

I stared at him blankly. He leaned forward. "We are applying for bail, Rita. You understand what that means?"

"When do I get out?" I demanded dully.

"Soon, Rita, very soon."

"Today?"

"No, no. It's Friday today; no way to get the application processed until Monday. But first thing on Monday we will. . . ."

"What will they do with me until Monday?"

Mr. Sorochai faltered. "Oh, they'll take you out to the prison."

"What's it like?"

He brightened. "It's better than here."

I was taken back to the corner cell, where I sat until six or seven in the evening, resolutely refusing food and drink offered me by different Thai girls. The heat was unbelievable. Normal Bangkok heat is bad enough, but the number of people in the cell made the temperature almost unbearable.

When it was time for the prison bus to leave, everybody began crowding toward the door. I decided I wasn't going to try to be among the first out. I had my cardboard box full of belongings, and I didn't want to get caught in the scrimmage that was developing. One of the Thai girls, seeing me hanging back, took my arm. "Come! You have to be at the front!"

"No, no!" I became quite nasty about it, but I was terrified and apprehensive. So I staggered after the crowd, carrying in my cardboard box the contents of James's three suitcases.

The most dilapidated van imaginable stood outside. It would seat about twenty-five in comfort. I saw now why everyone wanted to be first out. Everybody, young, old and pregnant, rushed to clamber on. I managed to find a place somewhere. As the van lurched off, I clutched my box and began to cry again.

"Don't cry."

It was the Thai girl who had spoken to me earlier. "It's not so bad out in the Monkey House, you'll see. Maybe there'll be something to eat when we get there. It'll be all right. Don't cry."

Eventually the hot cramped journey came to an end, as the van drew up at the Lard Yao Women's Prison. We stopped in front of an enormous pair of iron gates. It was almost dark. Somebody was opening the gates. We drove through, and they slammed shut behind us.

Everyone clambered out. A battery of bright lights blazed overhead, dazzling after the gloom of the van. I felt hot and headachy. We were in a small enclosure, bounded on two sides by walls, on the third by the gateway we had just driven through, and on the fourth by another iron gate facing it. The enclosure rapidly became chaotic as the prisoners spilled out, chattering and in some cases crying.

We were being marshaled into the semblance of a waiting line. On one side of the enclosure a desk had been set up. Two or three women in uniform began to organize us brusquely and efficiently.

"Everybody must surrender any cash or valuables in her possession." The announcement was made in Thai and English. Slowly, the disorderly file of people began to move past the desk, handing over money and personal treasures. I was in no mood to be cooperative. As my turn approached, I watched the Thai girl ahead of me handing over a single ring. She began to cry as it was labelled and disappeared from view. I stepped up to the desk, feeling very angry. The woman behind the desk pointed to my watch and some items of jewelry I was wearing.

"I'm not giving you these," I said emphatically. The officer was inflexible.

"*Mii* (Yes), you give it. But we pass it to your Embassy for safe keeping." My protests fell on deaf ears. Eventually I submitted, seething.

Our valuables deposited, we were herded out of the enclosure through a small door which was part of the big iron gates. We found ourselves on a pebbled path. I clutched the cardboard box which held my possessions and looked around. In the twilight, I could see trees surrounding a large compound, in which were several two-story wooden buildings. In the nearest of these I was searched again.

"Remove your bra and pants. You can put your other clothes back on." I was searched efficiently and very thoroughly. To add to the trauma, a stream of Thai prisoners wandered through while I was being searched, consumed with curiosity about whether a European woman was different from themselves.

These admission procedures only emphasized my situation. I was in other people's hands now; no longer the girl friend of a charming and wealthy playboy, on her way to spend a few all-expenses-paid weeks in England—but a prisoner, to be searched, ordered around, and told what she could and could not do. It was unbearable; I had reveled in money and freedom. As the dreamlike trance fell away and I began to take notice of where I was and what was happening, I was gripped by an icy fear. I had no idea what I had been sent there for. I didn't know whether I would be kept there for a long or a short time; nobody had told me.

The officials began to search my possessions. As I watched helplessly, a woman appeared, a plump bespectacled lady in nightdress and flipflop sandals. "I'm Hannah," she said, calmly and reassuringly. She began expertly to translate what the officials were saying. "You can't have that—that will have to go to the Embassy—yes, you can have that—and that—no, those will have to wait. . . ." One of the officers held up my contact lens case. In fluent Thai, Hannah explained what contact lenses were. When she had sorted things out with the officers, she took me across the grounds to another wooden building, where the prison kitchen was. "I'll get you a cup of tea," she said.

Hannah put the kettle on, and we sat down facing each other across a scrubbed wooden tabletop. The kitchen was a fair size, plain and unwelcoming, but the kettle boiling on the stove was a cheerful sound. I wasn't feeling very cheerful. Apart from anything else I was having difficulty keeping my eyes open.

"I'm Rita." I thought I might as well take command of the conversation.

Hannah nodded. "I know. We heard about your case when you were arrested," she explained.

I took another look at her. "Are you a guard or something?"

Hannah laughed a short, loud guffaw. "Fat chance! I live here. I'm a prisoner. Like you. Been here three and a half years."

I was stunned. My thirty days in the police cell had seemed like a life sentence.

Hannah got up to make the tea. When she sat down she resumed: "We figured you must have bribed your way out of it—most people get sent here after twelve days or so. Well, so here you are now. Heroin. You were the one with the heroin at the airport."

"Yes," I admitted.

"That's bad."

"Oh," I said, nettled, "it's not as bad as it looks. You see, they're not holding me on a drugs charge."

Hannah gave me an odd look. She spooned sugar into her tea. "And what exactly are they holding you on, then? They don't send people out here for nothing."

"Article 21. That's breach of peace. My lawyer's going to get me out on bail on Monday."

Her body shook with an enormous gale of laughter. "You silly little cow!" she roared. "Article 21? That's a Martial Law Order—everything from treason to traffic offenses! They can do anything to you under that order, *anything,* do you realize? 'Not as bad as it looks! . . .'"

I paled. *It's happened,* I panicked. *I'm here forever. I'm going to be shot. God, what's going on?*

"But I'm innocent!" The words came tumbling out frantically. "I didn't do it—it wasn't my heroin. I didn't know about it. You see, it was. . . ."

"Don't give us any of that stuff," said Hannah, not unkindly. "We don't want any of that. You're in prison now with the rest of us. We're all innocent in here. You ask any of us." She got up from her chair. "I'll show you where the washhouse is."

She produced soap and a towel. "You can borrow these." We went to the washhouse. Hannah indicated a long low trough, like a stone horse-trough. A pipe above one end trickled water. I couldn't see any taps. "There's no water in the trough," I said. She picked up a bucket.

"You fill this from the pipe, and you wash like this. . . ." She mimed pouring the water over herself.

It was only slightly less adequate than the dipper-shower in the police station. I was hot and sweaty after the journey, and was longing for a wash. Gratefully, I peeled off my sticky clothes. Clad only in my pants, I reached for the bucket. A snort from Hannah made me turn around. She was staring at me in vexation. "No, no!" she said. "That's not how you do it. You mustn't go naked. The Thais don't like it."

I didn't know about the extreme modesty of the Thai people, or that nudity is something that they avoid. I just got angry, ignored Hannah, and had my wash. "Stupid animals!" I muttered vindictively as I scrubbed myself. "There's no understanding them. We're all females together, after all." Hannah watched me glacially.

After my wash I felt a bit better, and Hannah didn't mention the nudity question again. She took me back to the kitchen and made another pot of tea.

"I'll see about getting you a decent place to sleep," she remarked as the tea brewed. "Some of them are worse than others."

I had no doubt that Hannah would be able to manage it; she seemed that type.

We finished our tea. I rubbed my eyes and yawned. "Come on," said Hannah sympathetically. "I'll take you to where you'll be sleeping."

I collected my cardboard box and followed her across the grass to another of the two-story wooden buildings.

A few guards were the only people to be seen. We climbed up the steps to an open-sided landing, from which various doors led off. Hannah opened one of them. "That's the room prisoners usually go in when they come straight from court."

It was terrible. It looked as though there were about a hundred women in the dormitory, sprawled on the floor, sitting talking, sleeping, or arguing. The heat was overpowering; though it was a large room, it was crowded. It smelled of too many hot people too close together.

Hannah laughed. "Don't worry. I've found you a better place." She took me to another room. It was smaller; there were less than thirty women in it, all Asian. They looked up in curiosity as I came in. Behind me, Hannah said, "Good night," and closed the door. I clutched my box like a shield and looked around.

A fat woman of about fifty got to her feet. She looked more Chinese than Thai. She was wearing baggy Chinese trousers and a blouse which struggled to contain her huge bosom. She was pointing at me. I stood uncertainly at the door. She gave a wide, gappy smile and said something in Thai. When I didn't reply, she advanced toward me, gesticulating.

"*Mama-san!*" She pointed to herself. The word is a useful Chinese expression meaning anything from a brothel Madame to the woman who supervises the girls in a nightclub. I knew the word well. I gathered she was in charge.

"Where's my spot?" I demanded harshly. The floor looked full of mats and blankets spread out for bedding. Each place was occupied. The Mama-san beckoned one of the Thai girls. "Spot?" she queried. The girl spoke rapidly in Thai. The Mama-san's frown cleared. "Spot!" she announced. "There!" She pointed to the far end of the room. "There—for you, there."

I looked at the three floorboards which were my bed. Next to them a really filthy woman was sleeping. Lice crawled on her clothes and her skin. Shuddering, I laid a few things on the floor for bedding and gingerly lowered myself down. The filthy woman stirred in her sleep. I turned the other way. A Thai girl in her twenties smiled at me and said a few words in her own language. I ignored her and stared at the ceiling, remembering the antiquated but effective fans that had hung in the police captain's office. Only a naked light bulb hung from this ceiling.

There was no way I could sleep. Angles of my body ached against the floor, and the other women touched me inquisitively from time to time. After a few minutes I felt a stinging pinprick in my thigh; it was my first mosquito bite. Horrified, I saw things crawling out of the gaps between the floorboards. I pulled a sweater from my box and wrapped it around my scalp. It only made the heat more difficult to endure.

The light was not turned off that night. It wasn't turned off any night, and for the whole time I was in Lard Yao, I longed for the luxury of a dark bedroom. That first night I had no defenses against the heat, the light, the mosquitoes, or the lice. Others in the room talked and moved around noisily late into the night. My body ached; I thought I would never be able to close my eyes, but tiredness won. Soon I was dozing fitfully, and by morning had fallen asleep.

8 Betrayed

*The crackdown on drug smugglers in
Thailand has come in conjunction
with an attempt . . . to re-educate the
hill tribesmen in the notorious "Golden
Triangle" of Burma, Thailand, and
Laos. . . . The Thai spokesman said,
"Now that the supply of opium and
other drugs from the Triangle is
drying up, smugglers have been
running drugs into Thailand from
other parts of the world."*

Lancashire Evening Telegraph,
May 31, 1977

I woke early, stiff but partly rested, despite the
numerous bites that covered my arms and legs. A few

of the others were awake. One or two smiled at me; the rest just stared, openly curious. The Mama-san was awake. She grinned broadly when she saw me, and said something to her neighbor, who turned to me when she had finished: "She says you are not to be angry about where you sleep. Very full of people now. When other girls go out, there is more room for you." The Mama-san nodded furiously. She took a small tin from her clothing and noisily inhaled a pinch of black snuff. Then she sighed heavily and relapsed into her thoughts.

I sat on the floor and examined the room. It was very spartan, with wooden walls and floor. At the end at which I was sleeping, there was a roughly screened cement trough and a Thai-style toilet. The occupants of the room slept surrounded by piles of clothes and various belongings.

Half an hour passed. Then there was the sound of doors being unlocked. Everybody rushed out. One of the Thai girls said to me, "You must take your things with you. Door not open after we go. What you need, you take." I hurriedly gathered everything together in my box. I was one of the last to leave; a guard stood ready to lock the door again when we had gone. I had no idea what I was supposed to do next, so I decided to go to see Hannah again.

In the daylight I was able to see the prison properly. It was about the size of a large football field. The block of offices in which we had arrived in the van the previous night was a two-story building, with the main gate in the center. I found out from Hannah that it contained various offices and interview rooms as well as the Warden's office. The compound itelf was surrounded by a thirty-foot wall topped by an electric fence. Houses outside the walls later proved to be guards' houses. The prison buildings themselves were grouped in a rectangle, separated by grassed areas and cultivated patches. Around the perimeter of the prison was an open sewer. Vegetables were growing nearby.

I found Hannah working in the kitchen. She nodded a greeting and waved me to a chair.

"What do I do?" I asked helplessly.

"Have you had a wash?" asked Hannah. I shook my head.

"You can use my things again. Can you find your way? Anyway, follow the crowd."

By the time I got to the washhouse the line of people had diminished. Standing at the entrance of the last in the line of toilet cubicles was a prisoner who was obviously in some sort of command; she was staring grimly at us, arms folded. When a prisoner tried to take an extra bucket of water, the stern-faced girl barked an order, and the attempt was abandoned. Nobody seemed to be taking very much notice of her. The Thai prisoners were more interested in giggling and pointing at me. One or two of them tried to start a conversation with me; I grunted noncommitally in reply. I was more discreet in my washing this time, reasoning that I may as well get through the weekend without too much aggravation if I could.

When I returned, Hannah made some coffee. While she was doing this, the heavy reverberations of a struck gong sounded in another building. "What on earth is that?" I asked.

"Breakfast time," she said. I looked out. From all sides, women were converging on the refectory. As the line formed, a chant of Buddhist devotions began—a rising and falling rhythmic incantation. Still chanting, the line shuffled forward into the room. Nothing would have induced me to go in.

"Not hungry?" inquired Hannah sardonically.

I shuddered. "I can't take it . . . all those people. . . . How long does the chanting go on for?"

"Oh, they quit after a while," she said. "Here. . . ." She placed bread, butter, and jam before me. "Not prison rations, I'm afraid. You'll have to fend for yourself if you want to eat like this all the time. Of course, there's the prison food. . . ." She gestured toward the refectory, where breakfast was now well advanced and animated conversation had replaced the chanting.

"What do they give you?"

"Oh, rice . . . vegetables . . . fish. . . . It's wholesome enough. Just not so interesting. Dull, in fact."

"Tell me what all these buildings are."

Hannah reached for a pencil and some paper. I munched bread and jam as she sketched. "I'll draw you a map . . . right. Now, here's the gate where you came in last night. Over here we've got Building No. 1. That's where the long-stay people are. Women with over ten years. Downstairs is the factory."

"Factory?"

"Sewing workshop . . . we call them factories. Building No. 2 is where the 'on trial' people go, and a few lucky ones who should be in Building No. 1. That's where you are. Downstairs is the laundry and the library—you'll find a few English books there. People leave them when they go out. Oh, and there's the beauty salon."

"What?"

"Oh, yes. Mind you, it's not cheap, and you can't depend on it. The results are unpredictable. You can use it if you've got the money. Just don't rely on things turning out how you want them. Now here is Building No. 3, where the light sentences go. Six months to a year, that sort of thing. Another factory underneath . . . and if they can't find space for you anywhere else, you go in Building No. 4. Not a good idea. The nursery's underneath."

Later when I visited the nursery, I saw what she meant. It was in the heat of the afternoon. Mothers were changing their babies, lines of cloth diapers were hanging up to dry, still more waiting to be dealt with, and there was a din of crying. The noise and the smell were awful. Thai people are clean by nature, but you can't fill a room with so many babies and expect it to smell nice.

Hannah added two more rectangles to her map: the hospital building and another sewing factory. She added a pond beside the hospital. "And that's it," she finished. "Lard Yao Women's Prison. Welcome."

Something was bothering me. "Hannah, you said I was on trial. You mean some kind of probation?"

She laughed grimly, removed her eyeglasses, and rubbed the bridge of her nose. It was a habit with her I'd already noticed. "They sure didn't tell you much, did they? You're on trial. That means your case is being heard before the courts. You'll go to goodness knows how many preliminary hearings and one day they'll tell you how many years you got. Then you're not on trial anymore. Then, you're sentenced. Now, you're on trial and you live in Building No. 2. OK?"

I gripped the edge of the table. I could feel the blood rushing to my face. "But I'm going out on bail next Monday. . . Mr. Sorochai. . . ."

Hannah shook her head in frustration. "Look, honey, face facts. There's no way you're going out of this place on Monday. They're not going to give you bail. That was one hell of a lot of heroin you were carrying. Three and a half kilos! There's kids in here that had fifty grams of the stuff. Their lawyers can't get them out on bail. Who's going to pull strings for you?"

My heart was pounding. "I'm English. I'm a foreigner," I stammered. "They can't do that to me."

"I'm German-American," said Hannah. "They did it to me." She laughed. "I wasn't carrying any stuff, either."

Monday came and went, and just as Hannah had said, no word came from Mr. Sorochai. I realized that it was going to be some time before things got sorted out. I remembered what Mr. Sorochai had told me about the slow judicial procedure in Thailand. Things looked very bad.

I worked the events of the past weeks over and over in my mind. As days turned into weeks, I pieced the story together. There was still no word from James. I asked Hannah what she thought, and she was characteristically blunt.

"You're a naive young fool," she said crisply.

"But it was Simon, not James. . . ."

"And James had never met Simon, I suppose?" asked Hannah sarcastically. "Don't be a silly goose, Rita. Face facts."

After a number of similar conversations I began to realize that, however much it hurt, the truth was that James had been involved in the heroin planting. I couldn't believe it at first, but gradually my thoughts began to alternate between stark disbelief and a cold certainty which, try as I might, I couldn't argue away. The comments of lawyers and Embassy officials visiting me provided missing pieces of the jigsaw. As the story sank in, I was forced to believe it.

James and Simon had set me up well and truly. During that long lazy afternoon at the hotel, while I was blissfully luxuriating, Simon had fixed the false bottoms into my holdalls and packed them with heroin. The young Chinese prisoner, Alan Soon, had been Simon's spy, flying on the same plane and keeping an eye on me to make sure that things were going as planned. His role was that of "escort"; I was the unwitting "courier."

In fact, it seemed, things had gone wrong from the start. Word had apparently been sent from the Hong Kong police informing the Thai authorities that we were going to Bangkok and would be attempting to leave on the Air France flight 193. I never found out what had led the Hong Kong authorities to send the message in the first place, though it was rumored that somebody had tipped them off.

The police had been waiting for us at Don Muang Airport; they searched Soon's suitcase before I went through the baggage check, but found nothing. He was taken into custody at the same time I was, which explained why he was in the room when my bags were opened.

After their arrest and detention, Simon Lo and Alan Soon were deported from Thailand as "undesirable aliens." It was said that they had bribed their way out of trouble. I believed it. I would have believed anything of those two. Well before it was all officially confirmed by my lawyers, I knew that all three men had used me without any thought about what would happen if I was caught. It was only the freak tip-off which had involved them in the arrest at all. I had been the dupe carefully chosen by James and cynically shepherded by Simon, the one who was to carry the heroin and, if necessary, to take the rap.

Strangely, my first anger was directed against myself. How could I have been so stupid? I was the one who knew about men, who could pick out the gropers and the charmers and deal with them expertly. I was the smart one, the traveler. How could I have fallen for such an easy trick?

Then my anger at myself passed, to be replaced by a bruising hurt. Was it possible, I asked myself incredulously, that James had been so loving and considerate, knowing all the time that he was going to use me like this? The answer had to be yes.

But I loved him! I cried, thinking it through in the long hot nights. Memories of other nights spent together, of embraces in the hills and good times in restaurants and clubs, flashed across my mind. Try as I might, I couldn't erase the memory of James's handsome, heartless smile. It was the one time in my life I have really understood the way a murderer must feel. I would have killed him. But he was back in Hong Kong, at the Kokusai, at all the places we'd been together, and I was locked in Lard Yao.

It helped to be angry; it was a vent for my feelings. But there were times when the anger was spent, and all that was left was a desolate misery. I'd loved James. We were going to live together. I'd built what hopes I had for the future around him. Now it was all finished. Now there was nothing except my family, and they were half a world away.

9   Jailers

*In the daytime it's not too bad, as
there are four other foreigners here.
. . . After I'm locked in at five PM,
I'm just with Thai women, and not
being able to speak and share their
jokes, is a bit lonely, and it's very rare
that anyone speaks even a few words
of English. So you see why I'm trying
to learn the language. I'm not doing
too bad, but I'm far from a conversation yet.*

Letter to Aunt Margaret and Uncle
Tom, July 10, 1977

I was gradually beginning to find out what was
going on. I received visits from the British Embassy,

lawyers, and various officials. It emerged that I would be dealt with under standard Thai legal procedure, which involved regular visits to the courts to comply with the "holding procedure." I had to sign documents each time which held me for a further period. My trial would consist of several appearances; at the preliminary hearing, the police would give their evidence. I would be allowed an interpreter, and I would be required to plead guilty or not guilty.

The preliminary hearing was set for June 6. If I got bail, at least I wouldn't have to sit it out in prison. *God,* I screamed silently, *why are you doing this to me?*

Just after the evening meal, I was sitting on the grass, watching the other prisoners. A few yards away a tall Thai girl, light-skinned and attractive, was squatting. She was working at a piece of embroidery, her hands drawing long delicate threads from a complicated design. She frowned as she worked and occasionally drew on a cigarette which she was sharing with another prisoner. Her name was Muur; Hannah had pointed her out to me. Muur's work ended up in the prison shop, where it was sought after for its fine quality. I had only said hello to her when I was briefly introduced. She spoke good English, but we hadn't much to talk about. Muur was in for twenty-five years. She had killed her husband with a table knife.

Seated near her was Waneeda. She was short and stocky. Her arms and hands were covered with crude homemade tattoos. She wasn't doing anything except smoking and vacantly looking into space. Hannah had pointed her out to me as well. Waneeda was a heroin addict. She had been in Lard Yao thirty times. She was twenty-eight.

There were many murderers and many addicts in Lard Yao. After a few weeks I didn't think twice about it, except for the frequent outbursts of violence and tension. In any case, I didn't want anything to do with my fellow prisoners. I despised the Thai people—not only the judges and police who had put me in Lard Yao and the guards who were now running my life, but also the ordinary people in the prison with me, whose different way of life and priorities made them targets of my scorn and anger. I wrote letters full of bitterness. I was critical of everybody who tried to help me. I scorned my lawyers, the British government and its representatives, the Thai authorities, and just about everybody else. I raged at them all: in letters home, in public at anybody who was within earshot. And I also raged at God.

I knew about God. I'd been to Sunday school regularly from the ages of four through eleven or twelve. My sisters and I went to a little chapel every Sunday afternoon near our home. Our parents didn't go, but we were regular attenders on Sundays and at the Girls' Club meetings during the week. One summer I had even gone on a Sunday school camping retreat. There I'd made a "commitment to Christ," as they called it. I wasn't very clear about it all—I didn't understand all the talk about being "saved"— but I was curious, and stayed behind after one of the evening talks to learn more. Despite my uncertainty about the details, I felt that something very important and worthwhile had happened. In addition to that, I was confirmed. This came about because a friend of mine went to the local Anglican church. When she began to talk about "being confirmed" and going to "confirmation classes," I thought, *That sounds interesting. I'll do that too.*

Yes, I knew about God. I was a law-abiding English girl, who tried to be a good daughter and not hurt anybody on purpose. I always considered myself a Christian. I continued to do so even after the Sunday school and church-going faded away as I entered my teens. I believed in God: he was basically good and kind, and preferred people to be good and kind as well. I believed in God as Creator of the universe, too; I couldn't go along with the theory that human existence was merely the result of an accident. The complexity of our own bodies denied that. I had a great admiration for Jesus Christ, too. Still, I didn't know very much about Christianity.

A faith like mine was scarcely enough to support me in prison. As I began to realize the full serious-ness of what had happened, the last shreds of my habit-formed Christianity fell away. All that was left was a fierce anger against God. If he existed—if he actually was good and kind as I believed—why had he allowed me to get into this mess? I hadn't done anything wrong; it wasn't my heroin in the bags. Why wasn't Simon in prison instead of me? Where was James at this moment? Why had God allowed him to use me as he had?

It's not fair! I shouted at God. *Why me? What have I ever done to deserve this? And what about James and Simon? Why have you let them get away with it?*

Outwardly I put on a brave face, writing to my

mother that "the bastards won't get me down, no matter how hard they try." Inwardly, I raged away.

Look at all these people! I stormed. *What chance have they had? Stuck in here. . . . If this is the way you run the world, I'm not interested. I don't want to know.*

To onlookers I must have seemed to be adapting fairly well to the prison routine; I kept myself clean and tidy, and I fitted into prison life quickly. I expected to be leaving soon, and I intended to keep myself in shape.

The worst thing was that there was no freedom of action. If you were supposed to be at a particular place at a particular time, you had to be there at that time. Out of doors it was pleasant enough. Often, sitting on the grass with the sun shining, I thought how unbearable prison in the middle of a city miles away from growing things would have been. But it was a prison regime, with tedium and rules. The problem with the rule books was not that they were rigidly enforced—quite the opposite. A rule could be rigidly enforced in one situation, and then be ignored in an apparently identical one. Sometimes you were allowed to leave your room at night for a while; other nights it was impossible—"against the rules." You weren't allowed to have eyebrow tweezers with square edges; they were a potential weapon. You were allowed, on the other hand, to accumulate as many glass bottles as you liked.

I attempted to argue with the guards at first.

"Of course I can have this box of chocolates. It was sent in by the Embassy. It's got my name on it."

"Not allowed" was the stolid response.

"But I was allowed to have the box that came in last week for me. If it's allowed one week, why isn't it allowed this week?"

"Not allowed, not allowed."

In the end I accepted that when they gazed at me with that blank incomprehension, there was no use trying to argue further.

The guards were always around. They varied from quite pleasant women to vicious disciplinarians. Some of them were feared. One known as The Motorcycle always wore blue sunglasses, whatever the weather. When The Motorcycle was around, you watched your step. She carried a swagger stick and used it.

"Nightingale to report to the interview block!"

The loudspeaker crackled imperatively. I had quickly become used to its continuous music interrupted by official orders. Thai people have a constant background of music in their lives; prison was no exception. I made my way to the gatehouse block, taking care not to walk too quickly. No point in seeming overly keen.

An elderly man was sitting in the bare office. As the guard opened the door, he rose to his feet with elaborate courtesy. The guard took up her position impassively by the door. The man shook hands gravely.

"Albert Lyman," he said. His voice was a loud Southern drawl. "Honored to make your acquaintance, Ma'am."

I blinked. He wore a lightweight suit without a tie. He was almost bald, and slightly stooped. He gestured elegantly toward the other chair. He seemed to have appeared from another century.

"Who are you?" I demanded.

He pointed a finger at himself. "I am the senior partner, Ma'am, of Tilleke and Gibbins. Mr. Sorochai is my colleague." He tipped his open briefcase onto the table between us. A sheaf of papers fell out. Peering at them with watery eyes, Mr. Lyman selected one and scrutinized it. "I have taken an interest in your case. A very great interest."

"When are you going to get me out?" My voice was harsh and tense. Mr. Lyman looked up in surprise.

"When? Why, as soon as possible."

"When's *possible?* Why can't I get bail?"

Lyman caressed his lapels. "My dear, it's difficult, a case like this. You must understand, many things are involved. Why, there are papers to sign. The police have to present their case. . . . It all takes time."

"Do you know what it's like in here?" The words tumbled out. "Do you think I want to be here one minute longer than I have to be?" The guard stood tranquilly at the door. I didn't know how good her English was and I didn't care. "There are thirty of us in that dormitory. I want to get out. Now."

Mr. Lyman sat back, his expression one of hurt surprise. "But we will get you out," he said. He rose to his feet. "We'll get you free, li'l honey!" he declaimed. "We'll get you outta here!"

He gathered his papers together. "You'll have a visit from Mr. Puttri. He'll be representing you in court."

"Puttri? Who's he?"

"Mr. Puttri Kovanonda. He is my colleague, and he is Thai. Consequently he is legally allowed to speak for you in court."

"I thought you were my lawyer." It was becoming impossibly confusing.

"Only Thai nationals are allowed to speak in court." He brightened. "But I'll be working on your case and preparing your defense. Yes, Ma'am, we'll get you out. Don't you worry about that. You'll be free soon. You'll be seeing a lot of me, li'l honey."

He grasped my hand and shook it warmly. Then he was gone. The guard stepped forward. We walked back into the compound.

My mind was a turmoil. I wasn't going to get bail; I wasn't going to be released immediately. I was going to have to go to court, and Albert Lyman wasn't even going to be allowed to speak on my behalf. *God,* I thought, *why are you doing this to me?*

By now I was writing home and receiving letters from my family. I filled pages with accounts of Albert Lyman, "an old American fool who is definitely gone senile." He later became one of my dearest friends. He was head of a leading law firm in Bangkok, and was widely respected as a lawyer. His only fault was that he misread my anger and tried to enthuse me out of depression. He tackled my case with a fiery crusading zeal, took an intensely personal interest in it, and veered between black despair and buoyant optimism as the court reports alternated between good and bad news. I knew none of this then, suffered him in frustrated silence, and struck up a better relationship with his assistant Leonie, who sometimes came to prison with the lawyers.

My life settled into a dreary pattern. The day began with the unlocking of the dormitory doors at six. Until five in the evening the dormitories were prohibited. Everything we might need during the day had to be taken out with us in the morning. Still in pajamas, I had to take my bag of toiletries, towel, and clothes with me. Every prisoner carried a similar bundle. That was one of the things that most got me down. A common complaint among the prisoners was that some had more things than others and were taking up too much space. But how much do you need to live? You had to carry any special food like a tin of meat or a packet of noodles. The Thai prisoners who didn't drink coffee didn't collect the morning ration of hot water and so were less laden. But everyone needed a bucket, or preferably two, for washing.

It was a gnawing grumble of prison life. Often, picking up my bundle of possessions yet again, I longed for somewhere to put it all. "If I had one little locker, just one, that I could leave things in!" But there were no lockers. When important visitors came and the prison was tidied up for their benefit, everything had to be concealed. Finding places was a perennial headache. In the end it was easier to pay another prisoner to find that "somewhere."

So, hot and sweaty and clutching our bundles, we were let out at six. The favored prisoners, who helped the guards and did various prison tasks, were let out first, which was considered a great privilege. When they had washed, the rest of us had our turn. There was a pitched battle as we struggled to fill our buckets from the pipe, but there was no alternative; it was impossible to do without the morning bath, the nights were so hot. Afterward, those who the night before had paid for hot water for coffee and ice for the drinking water went to obtain their order.

At about seven the loudspeakers began blaring Thai classical music and opera. This normal aspect of life in Thailand added to the general clamor of the prison. When there was a power failure one day, the loudspeakers were beautifully silent (and that night, with the light off in the dormitory, I had the best sleep I'd had for weeks).

Like other foreign prisoners, I never joined in the rush for the refectory as the gong struck to announce breakfast. There were two sittings for each meal, and over two hundred prisoners in each. I usually ate in the kitchen. Breakfast was bread and jam or something similar which I'd bought. As I ate I heard the droning of the chanted devotions, followed shortly by an uproar of conversation.

The staple diet provided by the prison was red rice, vegetable stew, and meat or fish. The meals weren't too bad nutritionally, and many of the prisoners grew fat on the rice, but to my prejudiced eye the food looked unappetizing. Also it was boring. The Thai prisoners supplemented their diet with food brought in by visitors, and I bought all my own food. I was able to eat fairly well. I had about 2,000 francs on me when I was arrested (about 200 US dollars), and that was put in my "prison account" when I arrived. The Embassy staff changed it to *baht* for me, and I was then able to use the prison bank, which issued a coupon currency valid at the prison shop.

This was a building in three parts. In one section you could buy toiletries, writing materials, and miscellaneous things like condensed milk. There was also a sort of delicatessen, which sold such things as bananas cooked in rice and wrapped in banana leaves and also unusual fruit like mangoes when in season. In a third part, cooked food was on sale, and it was there that I learned my first sentences of Thai. Each evening the menu for the next day was posted up and it was written in Thai. You had to turn in your plate accompanied with your order and retrieve it the next day. Each morning I found out how well I had translated the list the night before. Occasionally I bought myself a peculiar meal, but there were always plenty of people who would help to dispose of food which I didn't fancy.

Breakfast over, it was time to go to work. As an "on trial" prisoner, I wasn't required to work in the prison workshops. I worked with Hannah in the kitchen, making biscuits and cakes for the prison shop. It was a good place to work. There were plenty of tidbits. I paid a weekly sum to Hannah, and in return had my meals provided. Also, she was able to get various delicacies sent in from the outside. I didn't have to use the shop to buy food at all.

I got on quite well with Hannah. I'd never met anybody like her before. Characteristically pessimistic, she did not expect much of prison life, and as a result was fairly comfortable. She chafed constantly at the rules and regulations. She had been married in prison, to the man she'd lived with before her arrest; they weren't even allowed to kiss at the ceremony. Her husband was serving an identical sentence in the men's prison across the road. She was allowed to send him meals, but visits between them were out of the question. She had been very wealthy, but now her only regular income was an ex-serviceman's pension which her husband received.

I think she liked me because I wasn't a drug addict. I'm no great intellectual, but some of the girls who came in were so hung up on drugs that they were incapable of stringing any sort of conversation together. For my part, I found that Hannah's dour pessimism matched my own mood of bitterness. She tended to expect the worst out of life, and I responded to this.

Besides providing a good source of food, working in the kitchen solved one of the worst problems of my new life. It gave me somewhere to go during the day. That was another dreadful thing about being a prisoner. If you weren't working, there was nothing to do but sit around. The duties were straightforward. Each day there were tasks to be done for each day's cooking. On a good day they were finished at about half-past three. Prison lunch was at noon, but we usually grabbed ours when we could. Midday was chaotic at Lard Yao because the prisoners had to get what they wanted at the shop before two o'clock (or that day's issue of coupons became invalid), and then the lunch gong sounded. With over one thousand prisoners, the chaos was not hard to imagine. Hannah and I stayed well out of it.

When work was over, it was necessary to find somebody who would stand in line for you for the evening bath. Usually somebody would do this for payment. You could usually find somebody to do any prison chore for a small sum. By evening the water was less plentiful in the pipe, and it was essential to secure a place in line. This was a sociable time of day—after the evening meal when everyone had bathed, and was in her nightwear. For Hannah and me it was particularly good because we didn't have to line up at the shop for food. People chatted, sat on the grass, watched the numerous children playing, and generally relaxed until the gong sounded for bedtime.

Just before five o'clock the Thai prisoners had their evening devotions, which meant more chanting; and before reentering the dormitory, the prisoners had to sing the Thai national anthem. I kept my mouth firmly shut.

Because I was "on trial," I had no more duties after five. Those who had were called out to do things like cleaning the sewers or receiving new prisoners. That was what Hannah was doing when she greeted me on my first night. On weekends there was great excitement at six when the court van arrived, and those not locked in their rooms brought back news for the rest of us.

"Hey! There's another *farang* (foreigner) come in!"

A babble of interest:

"What's she like? How old?"

"Well, she's pretty, this one. . . ."

A guard was on duty in each building to let people

back in after their work, and by half-past nine everybody was finally locked in.

The day was over. Those who were able to, slept. The rest chattered or paced restlessly to and fro. Smoking was forbidden, but nobody heeded it, although fire was a constant fear. Nobody cared to contemplate what would happen to the prisoners locked in the wooden buildings if a fire began. Getting a light for a cigarette was difficult. I had a gasoline lighter, for which I stole fuel from the prison lawnmower. The usual method was to get a light from an adjoining dormitory by passing an unlit cigarette through a hole in the wall—the lighted one was never passed through to you, and by the time you got your own back it had been half smoked already.

The more tender-hearted guards often came up to the dormitories for a chat. It wasn't unusual to find them pouring out their troubles to you. Even though I was preoccupied with my own troubles and bitterness, I found myself feeling sympathy for them as they complained of hard work, low pay, and hostility. But I conscientiously refused to allow this to distract me from my anger. I wasn't their friend and counselor. They were still prison guards, part of the system I had sworn to resist. "The bastards won't get me down," I had written to my mother. And I was determined they wouldn't.

10 Maria

Wow! Are you well thought of here!
Your recipe for booze caused so much
excitement, we were all (foreigners)
dashing around madly stealing this
and that. Whatever it comes out like,
I assure it'll be drunk.

Letter to sister Ann, early summer 1977

Three beds away, two girls were embracing under a
blanket, oblivious of the crowded dormitory. I
hardly noticed them. I'd been in Lard Yao over a
month now, and had got over my first shock at
finding that lesbianism, as in any women's prison,
was common. I had more important things on my
mind than them. I was writing a letter to my mother.

My pen flew across the paper. There was a lot to

tell her. Balancing the pad on my knee, I scrawled furiously:

> The Consul came yesterday—what a performance. The Warden had us up most of the night cleaning, and yours truly was thoroughly briefed ... she's probably gone away thinking the place is a garden of Eden. I must admit the parts she saw, the garden and kitchen, do look nice; but the point is I'm not worried about conditions here. I just want a fair trial and to get out. . . .

I sighed and put my pen down. It was always difficult writing my mother. I wanted to reassure her I was all right, that she needn't worry, but also I wanted to tell her the facts, because I knew other people in England saw my letters.

I looked around. It was about seven o'clock. Francoise, a French girl I'd gotten to know a little, was combing her curly hair. I envied her for her looks. She was extremely pretty, with beautiful olive skin.

She saw me looking and smiled. "Tell them all about this terrible place, Rita." Her eyes widened in mock horror. "Don't leave anything out."

I grinned. "Not enough paper," I retorted. Francoise returned to her combing. Unlike many who came to Lard Yao, she was very sensitive and never pried into my background or why I was there. I picked up the pen again, grateful that Francoise had not asked whom I was writing to. I didn't want to talk about it.

I decided to finish the letter cheerfully; I'd sent enough depressing ones recently.

I've had a medical check-up. I had to go to the men's prison for it. What a treat to see males again! The guard was like a hawk, but I managed to get a few words with an English guy, who'd waited all morning to see me. He heard through the grapevine that the English girl was coming over. . . . My blood pressure's a bit low, but that's nothing. I had a chest X ray and gave blood samples and had my teeth checked. . . . Everything's OK, I'm sure. So don't worry. I'm as fit as a fiddle—at least I will be when I walk out of this place. . . .

I put the letter down and stretched out on my bed, flinging my arm over my eyes to shade them from the light. They were moist. *Come on, girl,* I scolded myself. *You don't have to let everybody know you're upset.* I wiped my eyes with my forearm. As I opened them again, Francoise glanced sympathetically at me.

Keys rattled. Standing at the door were a guard and a tall woman in her mid-forties. I remembered some of the girls saying earlier, when the prison van came, that there was a new foreign prisoner. The foreign prisoners were put in the better dormitories, where we were regarded by the Thai prisoners with a mixture of curiosity, fear, and envy.

The Mama-san was dabbing herself from a little bottle of green liquid, her favorite remedy for aches and pains. She stuffed the bottle into her pocket and shuffled to her feet. She greeted the newcomer, who stared at her blankly. The Mama-san tried a few words of English. The tall woman remained silent. She didn't respond to Thai or Chinese either. Francoise got up and gently took from the woman the box of possessions she was carrying.

"*Parlez-vous Francaise, Madame?*"

The woman's hunted expression cleared slightly. She nodded and spoke in a French accent even I could recognize as poor. "*Oui. Mais non l'Anglaise.*"

"*Comment vous appelez-vous?*"

"*Maria. Espagnole.*" As Francoise placed the box on the floor, Maria from Spain sat down heavily and stared at us all.

Maria looked sad and out of place in the dormitory. We were all in our nightclothes. She was wearing a floral print dress and high-heeled shoes. She was very neat, her short, thick black hair well styled. She was amply built, but carried herself well, with a regal air.

Francoise tried to draw her into conversation, but the only response was either silence or floods of Spanish. She was given a place next to mine on the floor. I was still in the place given me when I arrived—farthest away from the toilet. Maria looked incredulously at the bare boards. I gave her a blanket. Francoise tried to give some simple information about when we had to get up and so on, but didn't have much success.

As I dropped off to sleep that night, Maria was still lying with her eyes open, shifting restlessly. I tried to catch her eye and comfort her, but her gaze was fixed on something in her hand. It was a rosary. Her lips were moving silently as she passed the beads between her fingers. I shrugged and went to sleep. I had enough problems of my own.

"*Sodom y Gomorrah! Sodom y Gomorrah!*"

I sat up, panicking. Maria was wailing, her head

117

buried in her hands. *"Sodom y Gomorrah! Sodom y Gomorrah!"* she howled over and over again. The other girls woke up and complained bitterly. Françoise came over, but Maria would speak only Spanish.

Eventually we persuaded her to tell us what the matter was. Stuttering incoherently, she pointed a trembling finger across the room. Following her horrified gaze, I saw that the two girls were still in bed together. They were grinning, their arms around each other. Clearly Maria had only just realized what was happening. I laughed. "Just go to sleep and let 'em get on with it," I advised her drowsily. "It goes on all the time here. . . ."

Though I had gotten over my initial shock at the lesbianism in the prison, I never became used to it. I was often pestered by the more domineering girls. I didn't get involved because I wasn't interested. I couldn't believe how quickly—often in a matter of days—normal heterosexuals, finding themselves in an all-female prison, would strike up these relationships. Also I was so angry with everybody that I wanted no relationships beyond superficial ones.

Another unpleasant aspect of prison life was the number of prisoners who had serious drug problems. Most were inside for drug offenses, and there were always several undergoing involuntary withdrawal. You couldn't get heroin into our prison.

One night after the van had been there, a guard beckoned me from the door of the dormitory. "There's a French girl arrived. She will have to sleep in here."

"I don't speak French." I was unwilling to lose even a few feet of floor space in that crammed room.

"Doesn't matter." The guard was already bringing her in.

When I saw her, I thought, *This one's going to have a bad time.* One glance showed her to be a heavy heroin user. She was shivering. She didn't say a word to me, and my greeting was met with a resentful silence. I looked at Maria pleadingly; she could speak French. Maria sat rigidly aloof and avoided my eyes.

I found some bedding for her and generally offered help. Hunching into herself, she stared around with blank, tired eyes, and lay down.

There is a stench that comes from heroin users who are on withdrawal. It's like a wild animal's, as characteristic as the smell of death on a corpse. Anyone whose bed was near the new girl's moved as far away as she could. But the weird smell soon spread across the dormitory, hanging over us like a fog. Clean and neat herself, Maria couldn't stand it. She muttered fretfully in barely audible Spanish and retreated to a safe distance, watching the girl balefully.

For a few minutes the new girl lay rigid on the floor. Then she began thrashing around, kicking those within reach and waving her arms. A hollow ragged scream escaped her throat, cutting through the prison clamor, so that suddenly the guards reappeared. "Do something!" they ordered, as if by greeting the girl, I had become solely responsible for her. "What can I do?" I shouted back. "I can't speak French!"

She howled and thrashed for the next three nights, until we were exhausted and furious. In the daytime she was uncontrollable, but at least she wasn't in the enclosed dormitory. Having had some nursing training, I felt I should be helping her, but I didn't know what to do. Her sickness wasn't like flu or bronchitis. Eventually we had to ask the guards to put her in with other prisoners who had been through the same experience. Maybe they could help her.

So she was transferred. Her new roommates gave her cold water drenchings and sat by her for hours, thumping her rhythmically on the back with their fists. Apparently, it was an effective treatment.

After she and a few others had come to our dormitory and we had lived through nights full of their screaming, vomiting, diarrhea, and that inescapable stench, we begged Hannah to persuade the guards to put them in the large dormitory instead. We told ourselves that it was for their good, that they would be better looked after there. Full of gratitude to Hannah, we went back to our relatively peaceful evenings.

So far as I know, nobody died in Lard Yao from drug withdrawal. I often saw girls who were going through it. They couldn't control their legs, and looked as if they were on a bicycle. They couldn't believe that the authorities were not prepared to help them with drugs—not even an aspirin.

After a month or two such sights faded into the background, unnoticed and unimportant compared with the endless prison routine and the slow workings of the legal processes.

The Foreign Office had already warned that my case would be prolonged and complicated. The Thai government is under tremendous international pressure to take a hard line against drug smugglers because of its key position in the infamous "Golden Triangle" by which drugs are carried from their countries of origin to Europe, America, and beyond. Smashing the drug traffic at Thailand is an essential step in destroying the "Triangle" itself. It was not likely that my case would be pushed through quickly. The eyes of the world were on Thailand, and my plight was already attracting international interest.

If I thought about the problems of the Thai government at all, my anger made me dismiss them out of hand. The dominating thought in my mind was that I had been set up by three crooks, and I couldn't understand why I was in prison and they were not. I continued to vent my rage on every Thai I met. Toward the Thai prisoners I preserved an aloof coolness; toward the prison authorities I maintained a defiant rebelliousness and contempt. When I wrote letters home, I poured scorn on the Thai courts, their judicial system, and their lawyers. I called them fools and animals, pouncing on their faults and ridiculing them. I broke prison regulations. And once, when the prison censor held a letter in which I had been outspokenly and bitterly critical of the Thais, my contempt knew no bounds.

There were so many odd aspects to the story that I gave up trying to get the whole picture clear in my mind. A video film, for example, which had apparently been made of my interrogation, recorded my reactions to the discovery of the heroin. The film was described by journalist David Allin of the *Lancashire Evening Telegraph*, who was shown it privately when he traveled to Bangkok on behalf of the paper. The film, he told his readers, revealed my reaction of total shock and disbelief when the heroin was discovered, and was for him a convincing proof of my innocence. But when it was finally produced as evidence at my trial, that section had been inexplicably erased; the only image left on it was of me sitting in a chair, my head in my hands, the very picture of guilt. It was never discovered who had wiped the evidence from the film or why.

Mr. Lyman was confident he could get me freed. Having heard the other girls talk about their cases, I thought differently. I was sure mine was hopeless.

"I might as well plead guilty and be done with it," I told him drearily.

He shook a long finger at me like a schoolmaster. "Now why do you want to say a darn stupid thing like that?"

"The girls say that if I plead guilty, I automatically get my sentence halved."

"Sentence?" he bellowed. "Sentence? You ain't getting a sentence. We'll get you free, li'l honey, if it takes twenty years!"

I wasn't impressed. Hannah had told me that I could expect thirty years if I were convicted. Half of thirty was five years less in Lard Yao than Mr. Lyman appeared ready to accept. I turned on him angrily.

"Have you ever won a heroin case?"

"Ah. Well, I believe. . . . Hmmm."

"Have you ever won just *one* single heroin case in court?"

He looked downcast. "Well, no, as a matter of fact, it's true we haven't." He banged the table. "But yours is different! I do truly believe that we have a great case! And I won't hear talk of you pleading guilty, no, sir!"

June 6, the date of the preliminary hearing, drew closer.

The first letters from my mother and sisters after my arrest had made one thing clear. Whatever happened, they believed in my innocence, and were going to stick by me. I told them what I could in letters, and they rang the British Embassy and other government sources in Bangkok several times to find out more, until I begged them not to waste their money. It could aggravate relationships between me and the authorities, and in any case, we already had all the information that could be extracted. We would just have to wait.

In Blackburn, events gathered momentum. My arrest and imprisonment had been given national coverage in the British press, and our local newspaper, the *Lancashire Evening Telegraph,* began a campaign for my release, with David Allin's feature articles. *The Daily Mail* ran several articles about me. The British press were generally sympathetic. Even if I were guilty, it was argued, I should be brought back to serve my sentence in an English prison.

My mother was well loved in Blackburn, and the *Evening Telegraph* articles aroused great public interest. Letters, almost all sympathetic poured into the newspaper's offices. The Right Honorable Barbara Castle, our Member of Parliament, gave the case her close attention, though like the Foreign Office, she refrained from public discussion until the case went to court. In May it was announced that she had asked Foreign Secretary David Owen to find out what conditions were like in the prison. Dr. Owen did so and reported that I was being visited regularly by the British Consulate.

I saw none of the press coverage and picked up only a little of what was going on from letters and visitors. It was probably just as well that I did not see David Allin's story of May 31, with its headline: "JAIL GIRL *COULD* BE SHOT, SAYS THAI EMBASSY." Article 21 was wide-ranging in its powers.

In Lard Yao prison I gratefully absorbed the home news in the letters. Mother told me what she was planting in the garden and said that I must get back home in time to see the daffodils in bloom. My sisters told me all the ordinary everyday things that were happening. Eagerly I read about driving lessons, discos, and jobs. Ann's husband, John, sent a recipe for home-brewed alcohol which turned me into an overnight social success and made Hannah so alarmed that she poured it all away before it reached a drinkable state. I had a letter from Carl; he had stowed away on a Jumbo Jet and gone back to Australia. I inquired about the possibility of doing some studying while in prison. I even began to learn some Thai. It was best to be on the safe side. After all, I could be in prison for some time.

11   Court

*But I believe in fate and destiny, and
even our June in her letter said
everything is done for a purpose,
which is true, but not easy to face in
real life. What's hurting more than
anything, I will accept anything I get,
because it was my mistake. But you
and the family, what is it doing to
you?*

Letter to Mother, early summer 1977

The circle of girls and women were swaying in time
to a rhythmic chant. As I approached, I recognized
the Thai numerals. They were counting.

"Sii! (Four!)" A tremor of excitement passed through the crowd.

"Ha! (Five!)" The circle pressed closer.

"Hok! (Six!)" Intrigued, I pushed into the group to see what was going on.

A prisoner was standing against the steps leading up to the hut. She was gripping the rail. Her knuckles were white, her face screwed up with pain. Her thin sarong was hoisted to her waist. A guard was standing behind her, a stick raised to strike. The girl's bare buttocks and thighs were bruised from the blows that had already been struck. As the stick fell again, the crowd of prisoners watching took up the count again. One or two began clapping their hands in a slow rhythm, urging the guard on. Sickened, I turned away.

Beatings were common in Lard Yao. This one, I found later, was punishment for a fight. Dang was young and attractive, and was passionately devoted to a waiflike girl from the hill country who was also in Lard Yao. They were inseparable, and very demonstrative physically. The fight had started when Malee, Dang's girl friend, had shown an interest in another woman. The guard had found them fighting and was punishing Dang, who had a reputation as a troublemaker.

Dang was an intense person, and was often in fights. She had arrived in Lard Yao as the result of another relationship that had turned sour. She had had a girl friend who had been seen in the company of an American soldier, Dang's boyfriend, in Bangkok; they went into a hotel together. When they came out, Dang was waiting for them. She threw gasoline all over the girl, and then tossed a lighted

126

match. The girl burned to death.

Dang, when her temper wasn't aroused, was a peaceable girl, and was one of the quieter occupants of our dormitory.

By the time June 6 arrived, I had made up my mind that I was going to plead not guilty.

I had weighed the matter carefully. On the one hand, I knew that a guilty plea would mean an almost automatic reduction of my sentence. The sentence for heroin exportation was thirty years; a halved sentence with remission for good conduct would come to about ten years. My fellow prisoners told me I would be crazy to plead any other way. "You can't beat the system," I was told. "You're guilty unless you can prove otherwise in this country. How are you going to explain three and a half kilos? Who's going to believe you? Plead guilty and cut your losses."

As I saw other girls pleading guilty and returning from court with dramatically reduced sentences, I could see sense in what they said. After all, I reasoned bitterly, who cared what the stupid Thais thought? It made no difference what those fools of lawyers thought of my guilt or innocence. Once out of Thailand, I vowed, I was never going to set foot in the place again, and the sooner I was out the better.

On the other hand, I was innocent. It hadn't been my heroin. It hadn't been my scheme to try to smuggle the stuff through customs. To plead guilty wasn't just to say to the authorities, "Yes, I'm an international drug smuggler. I tried to smuggle all that heroin out of Thailand. I've been very wicked. Please be merciful." That was bad enough. A guilty plea was in effect to say to James and Simon and Alan Soon, "OK, I'll take the rap; you go free, I'll stay in prison." And that I wasn't about to do. It would be endorsed on my passport; I'd never be allowed into any country again. And what would it do to my family? They believed in my innocence. How would they feel if I pleaded guilty?

"You're a fool," said Hannah.

"Well, what would you do?" I demanded. "Go on. Tell me."

"I'd plead guilty like a sensible woman." We were in the kitchen, making Chelsea buns for sale in the prison shop. Hannah attacked the dough viciously with a wooden spoon. "Look, Rita, you haven't thought it through. You get fifteen years, and what happens? You're in your thirties when you get out. Earlier if you behave yourself. That's still time to make a life. Still young and pretty. Still time to find yourself a man who'll want you." She gave the dough a final, unnecessary thrust. "You get thirty years and what do you look like when you get out? Think about it."

I didn't need to. I'd thought about it on and off since my arrival. "I'm pleading not guilty, Hannah."

"But why? Tell me, why?"

I thought for a moment. "For the sake of my family. . . . Because I know I'm innocent. . . . And because if I plead not guilty, there's a tiny chance I'll win my case and walk out of that court back to freedom." As I said the words, I realized how idealistic they sounded.

Hannah banged her floured hands together. White clouds flew. She shook her head in bewilderment. "You've been reading too many fairy stories, Rita."

The days passed and merged into a blur. Suddenly it was only a few days to the preliminary hearing. I was told there was someone to see me. It was the normal visiting period with the usual crush of people. Suddenly I saw someone waving at me frantically. It was Shirley, who had been my companion when I'd first visited Hong Kong.

"I don't *believe* it! Shirley!" I shouted joyfully. "What on earth are you doing here?"

"I just arrived in Bangkok!" explained Shirley. "I've got permission to visit you every day!"

Seeing Shirley again made me deliriously happy. When she returned to Bangkok that day, she telephoned my mother and gave her a glowing account of how well I was looking, which cheered Mother up a lot. Shirley also went around various official departments, foraging for information about my case. It was the second good report my mother had had of me recently—the Embassy official from Blackburn, who had visited me at the police cell and also several times in prison, had visited Blackburn and while there had gone to see her. I wrote to her and told her how happy I was that Shirley was in Bangkok.

Correspondence with my mother, apart from being a precious link, often revealed interesting developments. Though I sometimes found it difficult to discover what was going on, the Embassy was very good at keeping her informed. Often the first time I heard about things was when she mentioned them in letters.

That was how I heard that attempts were being made to postpone the June 6 hearing to June 16.

"What's the idea?" I asked Mr. Lyman.

"Perfectly routine," he insisted. "We may need to get some more evidence. We have somebody in Hong Kong right now looking for Simon Lo. We may be able to force him to attend your hearing. So we're applying for a postponement."

"How many more times will it be postponed?" I said. "For how long is this thing going to go on?"

"It's just a matter of time. It all takes time," Mr. Lyman assured me. "Lo and Alan Soon have criminal records for drugs in Hong Kong. If we could find the pair of them, it could make all the difference. Your Foreign Office in London is very anxious we should make every effort."

"How long?"

"Well," he said carefully, "if all goes well, I don't see why you shouldn't be through with all this legal business by Christmas."

I would have been in prison nine months by then. The shock of this news was almost physical.

For Mother I put a brave face on things. "I'm all ready to face the court tomorrow," I wrote to her on June 5. "Nice cotton dress, clean hair, Shirley beside me, so best foot forward and head held high. . . ."

Next day, the hearing was postponed to July 12, and I had to settle down to wait again.

Matters moved forward. Back home, Mrs. Barbara Castle visited my mother and explained the steps that were being taken on my behalf by the British government. On June 27 I had another medical check, which proved satisfactory. I also had a further visit from Mr. Lyman. He was in high spirits.

"Remember I asked you to write to your family

and tell them that character references from friends and relations would help your case?"

I nodded. I had written the letter some weeks previously. I'd thought the idea was a pretty stupid one but followed through with it anyway. I shrugged my shoulders disparagingly. "So what?"

Mr. Lyman smiled broadly. "Well, will you look at these!" He dumped a pile of papers on my desk. "Character references! Here's a stack of people who believe in you, Rita, and they've written letters to prove it."

Numbly, I leafed through the letters. They were from friends in Blackburn and elsewhere; from people who knew me through my family; some from previous employers. Representatives of organizations in Blackburn had written. An ex-mayor of the town had contributed a letter.

I could only take in bits of what was written: ". . . Cannot conceive that she would knowingly be involved. . . . A girl of excellent character. . . . Nothing to suggest she would knowingly harm or hurt anyone. . . ."

Then I saw my sister Ann's signature.

I looked up at Mr. Lyman. My eyes were blurring. He was still enthusing. "Every one of 'em states that from knowledge of you, li'l honey, over the years, it's not possible you could have been involved in smuggling drugs. Here, look at this from the doctor. He says. . . ."

I walked unsteadily to a chair and sat down. He put down the papers, cleared his throat, and began to sort them into a pile, somewhat embarrassed. I regained my composure.

"Well, Mr. Lyman. . . ." I managed a smile. "I'll definitely be pleading not guilty. Can't let these people down, can I?"

"Attagirl!" exclaimed Mr. Lyman.

I was still bitter and angry. My lack of knowledge of the language and my ignorance of Thai legal procedure reinforced my willingness to see all things Thai in the worst possible light.

The Thais are a people whose culture is centuries old. Thai Buddhism, the national religion, is part of the oldest branch of that religion. The Buddhist ideals of moderation and virtue in all things underlie architecture, literature, painting, music, and everyday life. The present King and Queen, though their dynasty long since relinquished divine status, play a leading role in the religious life of the country. Despite the widespread influence of Buddhism there is religious tolerance, and under King Bhumibol Adulayev the country has gracefully westernized itself in many ways.

I had seen little of this in my travels, because I had spent only a short time in Thailand. On the other hand, I was well aware of the less attractive side of Thai society; I had seen the red light district side to which foreigners flocked, and I had heard there was an enormous trade in child prostitutes. My mind returned to these things as I brooded over the events of the past months. In other circumstances I would probably have conceded that my experience of the country was only partial, but I was anxious to believe the worst. I was living, too, in a prison, among thieves, murderers, and other criminals. I suppose I saw as little of the beauty of Thai classical culture there as the average English criminal in Wormwood Scrubs sees of Shakespearian theater.

I made it my business to be seen to be rejecting Thai customs and practices. I seized upon every fault and failing, taking them as proof that these people were just as I had said they were. There were beatings in the prison; I called the guards barbarians. Their food didn't appeal to me; I called it disgusting. Thai prisoners fought among themselves; I called them animals. I acquired a reputation as a trouble-maker, and it wasn't only because of the interest that was being shown in my case by the foreign press.

I made hardly any attempt to come to terms with cultural differences. There were frequent incidents in the dormitory. One night when I had only been there a few days, I woke up wanting to go to the toilet. We slept in two long lines the length of the room. Still a relatively new girl, I was sleeping in the worst part of the room, farthest from the toilet. I got up and made my way down the center of the room to the toilet, picking my way down the line of feet where the two rows met.

A few girls were still awake. I had already grown accustomed to sleeping despite the constant light, the muttered conversations, and the occasional fight. As soon as I started to walk, everybody flew into a rage. I backed against the wall.

"What have I done? What's the matter?" I couldn't make sense out of the shouts and gestures, but I was sure I was going to be physically attacked. One of the Thai girls who spoke some English tried to explain. "No! No!" she said, pointing downward. "In Thailand is no good. Feet! Feet!"

Apparently I had committed some serious social crime. I shouted back at them. "How do you expect anybody to walk across the room then? You can't tell me that in a room this size. . . ." I wouldn't back down. It's hard to preserve your dignity when everybody can see you in the toilet, but I walked proudly back to my bed, muttering, "Stupid Thais, how can they expect civilized people to understand them?"

The whole thing, when Hannah explained it to me next morning, turned out to be quite simple. In Thailand the feet are considered to be an inferior part of the body, and even to point your foot at somebody is considered insulting; you can easily offend somebody just by crossing your legs. Now I could understand why in the courtroom a guard had made me uncross mine.

I ran into trouble again when I decided to do something about my laundry. Where pretty lingerie was concerned, the natural curiosity of some Thai prisoners developed into theft. If you hung up a nice petticoat or bra to dry, you were quite likely never to see it again, or to see it in some other girl's possession. After a couple of such incidents I decided enough was enough; I hung my things on the wall of the dormitory over my head. Again, I was unknowingly insulting my fellow prisoners. My clothes were hanging above the level of the sleeping girls' heads.

I found it difficult to understand why some Westerners devoted time and energy to building relationships with the Thai prisoners. I was scornful of two in particular. Jack and Gladys Martin were American Southern Baptist missionaries who came inside the prison for an hour once a month, to meet the Thai girls and any other prisoners who wanted to see them. I used to go to their meetings occasionally, just to get out of the routine, but I thought the Martins were crazy.

"Those people look really happy!" I said mockingly to Hannah after I'd been at one of the meetings. "You know what that woman said? She said that if she were a prisoner in here, it would be all the same to her because God was in charge and he would still be with her!"

We both laughed and wondered what sort of a lunatic could say a stupid thing like that.

The character references from home softened my bitterness to some extent, and Shirley's visit made me almost mellow for a time. She was a visitor from my old life. She brought with her a generous gift of money from Bernie in Australia; that was another link with the old, free world.

Also, despite my bitterness, I was beginning to build some relationships in the prison. I had gotten to know Francoise superficially; I knew Hannah quite well; the foreign prisoners got on quite amiably with each other, and I was even on reasonable speaking terms with some of the Thai prisoners, especially those in the dormitory. And I loved children, of which there were a great many in Lard Yao. Some women had brought their children into prison with them. Others were pregnant when they had arrived, so there were scores of children of various ages.

One in particular, a pale-faced two-year-old, attached himself to me and followed me everywhere. He had been born in Lard Yao. When he was five months old, his mother was released. She left him in prison when she went out. He seemed fairly happy, calling about forty prisoners-"mother." They all fed and cuddled him, and he spent each night with whomever he had last been with that day. I often played with him, and we got on well.

In one way having somebody to care for made me more contented, but it also increased my bitterness against the Thais. Perhaps the mother had believed the child would have a better life in Lard Yao than outside; perhaps she knew he would be better cared for or loved better than she could manage. I didn't care. I chose to see it as callous rejection. "What animals," I asked savagely, "would do that to their own flesh and blood?"

It was another excuse to be angry.

An Englishman pushed his way over to me as I stood waiting for my name to be called. "Rita, I'm a journalist. Can we talk?"

It was July 12, and I was back in the courthouse. Mr. Lyman was with me, as well as his Thai colleague Mr. Puttri, who would represent me in court. The interview was short; I couldn't concentrate. When the journalist left he placed an envelope in my hand. "Press cuttings," he said. "Bring you up to date."

"I'll read them later," I replied, knowing I'd burst into tears if I looked at them there and then.

Mr. Lyman chatted to distract me. "You'll be before Judge Udom Tuchinda," he remarked. "He's a good judge. Ought to be—he studied law in England. His wife's English, too."

Mr. Puttri agreed, and they discussed the judge. I let the conversation flow over me.

Inside the courtroom the heat was stifling. A single fan suspended from the ceiling did little more than agitate the air. Although the proceedings were once again conducted in Thai, I was allowed an interpreter this time so I could understand what was going on.

The judge sat beneath an imposing portrait of King Bhumibol. Before the hearing began, he beckoned me and my lawyers to stand before him. He looked at me gravely.

"You intend to plead not guilty. I have to warn you that if you plead not guilty, and are then found guilty by this court, you will have incurred the full penalty." His English was impeccable. He stared at me before continuing. "A plea of guilty brings a comparatively light sentence," he concluded.

My body tensed. *The case is being prejudged before the evidence has been given. I haven't got a chance.* That was the only intepretation I was capable of putting on the judge's words.

Mr. Lyman became extremely angry. "This is just the beginning!" he cried. "We can appeal—take the case to the Supreme Court—even apply for a royal pardon!"

I was dazed and confused. The trial hadn't started and they were talking as if I'd been sentenced. Royal pardon? It was common knowledge in Lard Yao that the King had never pardoned anyone convicted in a heroin case.

We returned to our wooden bench. The hearing got under way. Five people gave evidence for the prosecution: three customs officers, a forensic officer, and somebody from the staff of the Asia Hotel. The

British Consul, hot and uncomfortable, took careful notes. Mr. Lyman sat by my side in barely controlled exasperation.

There was little to dispute in what was said. It was stated that heroin had been found in my possession. The results of chemical analysis were given. An account of my movements on March 19 was given. The judge sat in deep concentration, carefully writing everything down.

I was depressed and uncertain afterward. The next hearing was to be on August 19, when the police would state their case. There lay ahead several more hearings four or five weeks apart. In the meantime I would have to stay in Lard Yao. Knowing that I would have to decide quickly whether I was going to retain my plea of not guilty, I decided after agonies of indecision that I would not change my plea.

Infuriating to me, Mr. Lyman positively glowed with optimism as I became more and more pessimistic. My mother telephoned him that night. "It's looking good for her," he said. I couldn't see what possible grounds he had for saying that.

I wrote to my mother myself the next day, but the letter was so depressed and black-spirited that I decided to write another, more cheerful one afterward. Before I had begun the second letter, I had some amazing news. Mother was coming to Thailand to see me.

12 Mother

I could get forty years . . . what peace
I can find with a forty-year sentence
only God knows. . . .

Letter to Mother, September 17, 1977

"She's coming here, Leonie, to Bangkok; I can't believe it!"

Leonie, Mr. Lyman's assistant, was visiting me to sort out some legal problems. My mother's letter had arrived a few days before.

"We were going to have a holiday together next year in Australia. I suggested we could use the money instead for her to come here," I told Leonie.

"Seems sensible," said Leonie.

"Yes, but the amazing thing is that we won't have to use that money. The *Lancashire Evening Tele-*

graph—that's our newspaper in Blackburn—wants to fly Mother here with David Allin."

"The journalist?" I'd shown Leonie some of David's articles that my mother had sent.

"Yes. All expenses paid, there and back."

I wrote my mother saying how thrilled I was: "I'll be waiting at the prison gates!" I wrote a rather different letter to my sister Ann:

> "I know it's going to be very emotional for us both. . . . At the moment all I feel like doing is breaking down and sobbing my heart out on her shoulder. Oh, to go back to my childhood and tell her to make everything better. . . . I just want to go home. . . ."

Though I wasn't in bad shape physically and was adapting to prison life, I was begining to feel mentally drained after the tension of the past months. The boredom was still a terrible problem. I asked Mother to bring me some European magazines to read; anything to pass the time more quickly. A very kind letter from Barbara Castle encouraged me. I had spent a whole day laboriously composing a letter to her, and I had (rather diplomatically, I thought) poured out all my grievances. Her reply held out no earth-shattering hopes, but it was a compassionate and positive letter, and it cheered me up. With Mother coming to see me as well, things looked a little more cheerful.

She left Blackburn for her 8,000-mile round trip on August 13. "I am going to Bangkok," she told reporters, "on a wing and a prayer." The Mayoress of Blackburn wrote to her assuring her of "the love, prayers and hope" of everybody in the town. Mother had a gruelling schedule, with visits to the Embassy and other places in Bangkok, as well as visiting me in prison and going with me to court on the nineteenth.

Feeling desperately anxious to see her again, I began to make preparations for her arrival. I baked some special biscuits for her and got my nicest clothes ready. I didn't put on any makeup the day she was due to arrive, because I knew I'd cry all over it.

We were to meet in the "lawyers' room." This was considered a privilege. Ordinary, unofficial visitors waited in a large crowd before being admitted into a sort of enclosure near the main gate. The side of the enclosure had been made into a tall barrier. Facing it about seven feet away was another barrier, an enormous metal grille. This was the wall of the prison room into which those of us with visitors were sent. Visitors had to shout across the gap, competing with all the others clamoring to be heard. Visitors were usually allowed ten minutes or so.

For official visitors, lawyers, Embassy staff, and also those visiting prisoners who had any kind of influence, the "lawyers' room" was available. This was a bare room with a grille bisecting a table in the center. The visitor sat on one side, the prisoner on the other, and conversation was through the bars.

The two guards who accompanied me to the lawyers' room when my name was called were intent on everything being done in a law-abiding fashion. I was marched briskly to the door of the room.

Mother was sitting behind the grille. She looked

tired and frail. Somehow she seemed very little, as if she had been shrunk by the inhospitable room. Leonie was with her.

I pushed the guards aside. They tried to stop me, but I was already running past the grille. I flung my arms around Mother, and we both wept and wept. Dimly I was aware of the guards protesting behind us, trying to separate us, and Leonie explaining the situation in Thai: "It's her mother, do you understand? It's her mother. . . ."

Eventually we stood back and looked at each other. Mother found some tissues in her bag. I wiped my eyes and produced a watery smile. I went around to the side of the partition I was supposed to be, and we held hands through the wire grille.

We talked of anything and everything. People back home, family, friends, my case—it wasn't important. Just being together was what mattered. The hour we had been allowed seemed like minutes. Finally we had to part.

"Rita tells me you have permission to visit each weekday, Mrs. Nightingale," said Leonie. Mother nodded.

"Leonie," I said urgently, "make sure they understand—if Mother's here with a paper from the Embassy she's allowed to see me here, not in the visitors' enclosure. You must make sure they know. You must."

"I'll make sure they get the point," promised Leonie.

It was heartbreaking to say good-bye that first visit. But I left the room knowing I would see her the next day. Next day, however, things began to go wrong. I waited all afternoon for my name to be called. Then just before evening I was summoned, not to the lawyers' room but to the visitors' enclosure. I stormed in protest.

"You can't! She's my mother! She's come all the way from England, and I'm not going to shout at her across seven feet of empty space! She's entitled to see me in the lawyers' room."

My arguments were useless. In the end, it was across the seven-foot gap that we met for the second time. There were no other visitors there. It wasn't a normal visiting time. The guards watched us as we talked the best we could. I longed to reach across the gap and take her hands in mine. I was almost glad that we were allowed only fifteen minutes.

That night I went to see the Warden. I had not made a good impression on her, both because of my attitude to Lard Yao and because of the press coverage my case was getting. Nevertheless she listened to what I had to say. I lost control of my emotions and poured out all my misery and frustration. "And the guards won't even let me touch her. She's entitled to see me in the lawyers' room."

She regarded me severely. She was about forty, and dressed expensively. Her clothes were of the finest quality material, her shirts silk. On her finger she wore a ring with an enormous diamond. As she talked, she fiddled with the stone perpetually.

"It is not possible to use the lawyers' room."

There was no arguing with her implacable authority. Inside, I crumpled up.

"I can, however, understand how you feel." She paused, her fingers manipulating the big diamond.

"I think it would be in order if you sat between the barriers. Then you could be close to your mother. It will not be necessary for you to shout then."

Next day, carrying a cup of iced coffee for Mother, I entered the gap. They'd given her a chair to sit on, and she was sitting there looking forlorn in the empty enclosure. When she saw me she brightened. We talked again. Each day for the rest of the week we met like that until the day came for her to leave.

I wish I could say that I cheered Mother up, that I lightened the burden of her sorrow by being happy, positive, and contented. But I didn't. Instead I poured out my own sadness, and, try as I might, I couldn't hold back the floods of tears. Merely seeing her unlocked something in me. I'd been writing to her every week, sharing my hopes and fears, but now that she was actually here I wasn't allowed to embrace her and this made my imprisonment seem more than I could bear.

When she returned to England, she decided not to come to Bangkok again. She couldn't erase that first stark picture engraved on her mind, of me in the interview room—tear-streaked, watched by guards, fretful, and angry. It seemed to her that nothing could change it. She couldn't stand the thought of seeing my misery. Instead she waited faithfully for the day when I would be released.

The day we said good-bye I gave her a cake I'd baked on which were the words "I love you, Mother." She took it from me; our hands were trembling. She walked slowly away. At the door she turned and looked back, waved, and was gone. I ached for her. I wondered whether I would ever see her again.

Mother's visit inspired me; she was the visible goal of my efforts to be released. I even allowed myself a certain amount of optimism. But as September approached, I began to sink back into gloom. I allowed myself to become withdrawn, obsessed with my troubles. A flow of visitors found me sullen and uncommunicative. Lawyers, officials, and Embassy staff were all greeted with silence or rudeness. I wasn't much more agreeable when others came to visit.

One day my name was called on the loudspeaker. "Visitor for Nightingale!"

I made my way to the visiting compound and scanned the faces of those waiting. I didn't recognize anybody I knew. Two women, pressing against the barrier to see better, were looking at me excitedly. One was a pleasant-looking woman in her early forties; the other, an elderly white-haired lady.

"There she is!" the younger of the two exclaimed, and waved at me. "Hi! I'm Lucille Lunceford, and this is Margaret Cole."

"Hello," I replied, as civilly as I could manage. I wasn't feeling very sociable that day.

"We saw your photograph in the newspaper this morning."

I scowled. *I'm like an animal in a cage,* I thought.

They held up a paper bag. "We brought you some fruit," smiled the old lady. "We'll send it in for you. I hope you like pineapple."

Feeding time at the zoo, I thought bitterly. I succeeded in smiling. "Thank you," I called. It was difficult to converse. Other prisoners and visitors were talking on either side.

"We read about your case," said Lucille Lunceford sympathetically.

"I was used as a drug-runner," I stated flatly. "But you know that. It's in all the papers."

There was a pause. On my right, a visitor was arguing heatedly in Thai with one of the prisoners. I grasped the bars and tried to think of something to say.

"Why have you come to see me? It's a long way out of town." I hoped that didn't sound quite as insolent to them as it sounded to me. I was trying to be polite, to make conversation for a few minutes until I could decently leave. "What brings you out here?"

"We were praying together, and the Lord told us to come and see you." The way Margaret Cole said it, it was the most normal thing in the world.

Oh, no; the Godsquad. Visions, even, I groaned to myself. *What are these nutcases talking about?*

"Oh, thank you, that's kind," I stammered. Silently, I was raging at them. *Don't you know what's happening to me in this place? Don't you know what's happened in my life? Christians are on another planet. Fine in church, but in the real world!* . . .

Margaret Cole was speaking. "We came because God told us to. That means he cares about you, Rita."

At least she talked about God in a normal voice. She hardly sounded religious at all. The way she talked, he was a real person. Unfortunately, I knew better. A few months in Lard Yao prison and you knew whether there was a God or not. *Don't give me any of that stuff about God loving me,* I warned silently.

Aloud, I made a lame response. "Yes, I'm sure you're right." Margaret Cole looked at me perceptively and changed the subject.

Soon their time was up. "The cheek of it! Coming to a place like this and telling me God cares for me! They won't be back in a hurry," I said to Hannah later. "They've done their good turn for the day."

"You shouldn't get so worked up," Hannah remarked philosophically. "I like pineapples, even if you don't."

Mr. Puttri brought news of a sort. "I have heard that Wong and Lo and Soon have been arrested," he said. I sat up.

"Why, that's wonderful!" I said.

"But I have heard also that they are still at liberty. Some say one thing and others another. It is hard to know."

"Perhaps it's true. If it isn't, they might be arrested before long."

"You must not place too much hope on that," said Mr. Puttri. He shook his head mournfully. "If they are arrested to go to trial in Hong Kong—which is only a possibility—and if, in that trial a sworn affidavit is produced—which is again only possible—then there is still no guarantee that such an affidavit would help you in any way."

"But it must do!" I protested. "An affidavit would make all the difference."

"In such a case as yours it would make very little difference," said Mr. Puttri sadly.

I was furious. I had been counting on some sort of written reinforcement of my story coming from Hong Kong. "Anywhere else in the world an affi-

davit would have gotten me released!" I stormed.
"But not in crazy Bangkok, oh, no. The judge won't
even read it here!"

Mr. Puttri bowed stiffly and left me to my rage.

It was becoming evident that Mr. Lyman's esti-
mate of a verdict on my case by December at the
earliest was accurate. The preparation of my defense
was taking time. Crucial evidence in my support
was being sought, the British government was making inquiries, questions were being asked in Parliament. In the press David Allin raised the matter of
the unexplained deletion in the Custom Department's film. He also did some private research on
Simon Lo. Odd things happened that I didn't hear
about. While David was in Bangkok with Mother,
he had been approached by someone straight out of
a cheap thriller—a man touting for a rival law firm,
pouring scorn on Tilleke and Gibbins, and trying to
bribe David to influence me into changing my lawyers. A big case like mine was presumably a profit-
able thing to be involved in.

But I was not the only one whose case was making
slow progress. There was something odd about
Maria's. She'd been to court once or twice when she
first arrived, just as I had. But for a long time she
hadn't been called to attend. Things seemed to have
ground to a standstill. Nobody spoke Spanish at
Tilleke and Gibbins, which was also representing
Maria. Often when I was being interviewed by
somebody from the firm, Maria would be sent
through, too, because they were her lawyers; but she
became very frustrated. "No understand! No understand!" A woman who visited her from the Spanish

Embassy spoke to her only in Spanish, so I didn't get much of a picture of what was going on.

Then the visits from the lawyers stopped, and the Embassy didn't contact her anymore. Eventually we heard that an announcement had been made on the radio about Maria. She wouldn't be going to court anymore, ever. She had already had sentence passed on her under martial law. She had been sentenced to life imprisonment.

"You've got to tell her, Hannah."

A group of us were discussing the situation. Hannah agreed. "Looks like nobody else is going to."

We watched the conversation from a distance. Hannah was speaking forcefully, emphasizing her points with sweeping gestures; Maria was listening with a frown of concentration, straining forward as if by listening very hard she could make the words easier to understand. She had a polite smile on her face. Obviously she wasn't taking any of it in.

Later we made a concerted effort to explain matters to her. Picking our words from the scraps of Thai and French we had in common, we strung phrases together into statements which sounded bald and peculiar. How do you tell a woman of that age, who thinks she's going to get a short sentence or even be released, that she's been sentenced to life imprisonment—which in Thailand is one hundred years? Maria sat listening, her fingers working away at her rosary. "Life," we repeated. "They've given you life, Maria."

Either she didn't understand or she wouldn't take us seriously. "No, no . . ." she protested good-humoredly. "You're crazy, crazy."

But as the weeks went by and it became clear she wasn't going to court like the rest of us, it seemed that the reports had been true. She had been given life.

"This is Chris," said Hannah one day.

"Hi, everybody." Chris was a striking blonde, tall and thin and Dutch.

A new foreigner arriving in prison was an event. "What happened?" I asked. Chris grinned. "Caught at the airport. Well and truly. Had the stuff taped to my body."

The method was a well-known one. If you weren't body-searched at customs, you could walk through carrying anything you wanted, usually in plastic bags stuck to your midriff with surgical tape. If you did get searched, you were done for. There was no way out. The rewards were considerable, the risks worth taking, I was told by the several girls in Lard Yao who had tried to gamble and failed.

Chris put her things down. "Wow!" she said, thumping the floor. "Some bed!" She looked around. "Won't get lonely, anyway. . . . What's your name?"

"Rita."

"Oh, I read about you in the newspaper. Heroin, wasn't it?"

"That's right."

Chris smiled. "Mine was supposed to be heroin. I was sure burned. I was supposed to be taking this heroin through, you know? So when I got caught, I told them what it was and they were really heavy. Said I'd get a long sentence, all that sort of thing."

I grimaced. I knew the sort of thing.

"Well, they analyzed it, and you know what? It

wasn't heroin at all. It was morphine. I'd been taken for a ride. I couldn't believe it. The guy who sold me the stuff really ripped me off." She smiled, reminiscing. "Worked out well for me, though. They tell me morphine carries a much lighter sentence than heroin. It's an ill wind."

Though Chris appeared to be extraordinarily stupid as a drug dealer, she was very clever in most other ways. She learned Thai incredibly quickly, found her way around the prison in no time at all, and endeared herself to the Warden and guards because she was a workaholic, often working an eighteen-hour day.

At first I didn't see much of her, and in any case was not in a mood to make friends. She began to work in the kitchen with me, and despite myself I found myself liking her. She protected me against the more masculine girls. When any of them made advances to me—which happened from time to time—I only had to threaten to call Chris and they would back away.

"Chris, you don't have to stick up for me all the time, you know," I said more than once.

"That's OK, Rita; you're my mate," Chris would reply with her easygoing smile.

Even Chris's arrival failed to shift my black depression. I kept to myself most of the time and refused to be a model prisoner. I refused to give the guards the correct courtesy greeting. I insisted on speaking English to them and would pretend not to understand even when I could make out what they were saying. I was a loner, and when the official holidays brought days of classical dancing and games, I sulked in the dormitory. I questioned the guards' rulings and generally made trouble wherever I could. They often threatened terrible things that would happen when I was finally sentenced and the world press lost interest. "You wait till you're sentenced, and then. . . ."

I continued to write angry letters home, interrupted by occasional moments of cheerfulness when some sequence of events encouraged me. Hanging over me the whole time was the prospect of a sentence which could not be less than five years and which was beginning to look like thirty, forty, or fifty. I calculated the odds against a not guilty verdict to be astronomical.

I chafed at the Thai system of evidence, which seemed to me to give the accused no chance. On those rare occasions when I conceded that my lawyers were in fact very good and the judge a distinguished member of the Thai bench, I fixed on the fact that my lawyers' impossible task was to convince the court that three and a half kilos of heroin—worth nearly three-quarters of a million English pounds—had come into my possession without my knowledge or cooperation. As one of the customs officials had remarked to me, "That is an awful lot of heroin."

A fifty-year sentence seemed, likewise, an awful lot of time.

13 Plots

I will never plead guilty, and I now think I've been a fool to keep getting that idea in my head. . . . Mr. Lyman is really going all out to win this case.

Letter to Mother, September 21, 1977

"I'm going to write to my mother."

"And what d'you intend to say to her?" demanded Mr. Lyman.

"I'm going to tell her the truth. She's only fooling herself with false hopes. She'll be shattered when I'm sentenced. She ought to know the facts. I'm going to give them to her."

"And what are the facts, might I ask?" A dangerous gleam had appeared in Mr. Lyman's eye.

"I'm going to be given a big sentence." He groaned

and began to speak. I continued. "And when they give it to me, I'm not going to appeal."

Mr. Lyman banged the floor with his stick. "Not make an appeal to the High Court? Why on earth not?"

"Because it will take a year to process the appeal. Because I don't believe there's any chance of a sentence being quashed anyway. Because if I'm going to get out of this place, Mr. Lyman, it won't be through these endless court appearances. It will be because England and Thailand sort the thing out between themselves."

"And how do you think they'll do that?"

"They can pull strings. They can work behind the scenes. I'm going to create such a stink in the press that they'll sit up all night to get me out faster."

"It might not be that easy," Mr. Lyman said. His eyes were sad. Leonie, who had not spoken, reached through the grille for my hand.

"Please, Rita," she pleaded, "think about it. You won't lose by appealing. You don't even know that you'll be sentenced. . . ."

I laughed a short, humorless, wobbly sound. "No, I don't. But I will be. You know it's true. God himself couldn't get me out of here now." I laughed again. "Especially God."

My next court appearance on September 26 was, Mr. Lyman reckoned, the last before I would be called for sentencing. I slid into a cynical despondency, mistrusting everybody from God on down. I hated my lawyers; I now believed I should have pleaded guilty in the first place and that they had persuaded me against doing so. But since I had pleaded not guilty, I was going to stick to it. I reacted angrily to Mr. Lyman's and Leonie's suggestions that I should now think about changing my plea.

"There's still time," said Mr. Lyman. "You can plead for leniency."

"That's for cowards," I snapped. "It's my life, not yours, and I'll do what I want."

Patiently, Mr. Lyman explained the situation, ticking off each point on his fingers. "There's hardly any chance of finding any evidence about Lo and his friends. We've got the testimony from the bellboy at the Asia Hotel. It's not going to be of much use." (This had been a blow. We had placed great hopes on the statement of the bellboy, who had since my arrest entered the Buddhist monkhood. Our hopes were sharpened by the difficulty of extracting the statement. But he had said nothing to point to Simon and James.) "All the press hooplah isn't making the Thai authorities look any too kindly on you. Your Mrs. Castle in England has made 'em wary too, simply by asking questions she's perfectly entitled to ask. You have to understand that the Thais are very awkwardly placed. After all, the West has told them long enough not to be lenient on drug smugglers. They're under a bit of a spotlight."

It was a week after the two women had been to visit me. I heard different prisoners being summoned to the visitors' enclosure and wondered idly whether I would have any visitors that day, apart from officials and lawyers. It had been such a wonderful surprise when Shirley had come. I could do with more surprises like that.

It was Thursday, my day for visitors. They were

allowed into the prison by a special order of days allocated according to the crime committed by the person they had come to see. Food brought in from outside was usually shared. Smart prisoners chose their friends so that one was a murderer, another a thief, and so on. That way there was a constant supply of tidbits through the week.

After Mr. Lyman and Leonie had left, I heard my name being called. A visitor! I went over to the enclosure. There, pressed against the barrier by the usual crowd of people were Margaret Cole and Lucille Lunceford.

"Hi!" said Lucille. "How are you today?"

My heart sank. "All right," I volunteered. She held up a bag of food. "We're sending this in to you," she said. I felt a bit better. I could always make use of food. I'd better be nice to these people. Anyway, they were only allowed ten minutes.

"What's life like in the outside world?" I asked.

Margaret's face lit up. "Well, now, God is really doing wonderful things. You should see the children I'm working with. They are refugees from Vietnam. We've seen so much blessing."

It was as before; she was talking about God in a perfectly matter-of-fact way. As she and Lucille talked on, I became curious. Margaret Cole was an old lady with white hair, but she was doing a job which a younger person might have found strenuous. Lucille, too, seemed to lead a hectic life as a teacher.

"Why are you doing this?" I asked Margaret. "Why do you work in that transit camp? Why have the two of you come to see me again?"

"Because God told us to. And because we want to," they replied.

"You don't need to," I said violently. "God hasn't bothered with me so far. He didn't stop my being arrested. He didn't step in when I was left to take the rap for the guys who set me up."

I paused, embarrassed. After all, they were only being kind. "Sorry," I said quietly. "You just don't understand how it is in here. God hasn't done anything for me. If there is a God, he's left me in this place to get on with things. He doesn't come in here."

"But he has, Rita," Margaret said softly, barely audible above the raised voices of the other visitors. "He told us to come here."

Tears started to my eyes. "It's easy for you," I replied. "You're free."

After that visit, I began to feel extremely lonely. I dwelt on the fact that no heroin case had ever been dismissed in the courts; acquittals were snatched from the accused when the public prosecutor lodged his automatic counterappeal. I had bouts of homesickness, and sometimes woke crying from dreams of Blackburn.

Margaret Cole and Lucille Lunceford had left, promising to visit again. When they appeared the next week, I found I had actually been looking forward to their coming. When they asked me how I was, I told them. "I'm lonely and I hate being here."

The odd thing about them was how ready they were to talk about God. After three visits I had begun to respect them; they were remarkable people. But I was disconcerted by their openness. I wasn't used to hearing God talked about on weekdays. In fact, it was a long time since I'd heard him discussed much on Sundays. It struck me as being in rather bad taste. But when I was with them, it seemed the most natural thing imaginable to listen to their stories of how God had done something special for them that week or to hear them quoting Bible verses which they thought I would like to hear. When Margaret talked about Jesus Christ, it was like talking about a close friend. In some weird way, her experience reached out and involved me as well. I asked her, "Why do you come, really? I can sense— it's, well, like you love me in some way. Why would you want to love me?"

Margaret smiled. "That's the love Jesus has planted in me," she said gently. "And it's projected through me, to you. God loves you, too."

I must be getting soft, I thought to myself. *I'm swapping pious thoughts with a missionary.*

When they were gone, I felt warm and almost contented for an hour or so. Then it wore off. I told myself I shouldn't be stupid. It would take more than religious talk to sort out my problems. I brooded on the forthcoming sentencing, going over and over in my mind the things I'd heard from the other prisoners and the lawyers. It was all too complicated. So many hopes, so many promises. And now I was facing what could be a fifty-year sentence.

I wrote endless letters home, full of desperate attempts to pull off a victory against what I believed to be only a relentless machine, the Thai judicial system. I knew nothing about English law, let alone Thai law, but I was convinced that I was being robbed of my rights and dealt with inhumanly. I would hear no arguments otherwise. My mind was made up.

I wrote to an Interpol officer, shrewdly composing the letter to give the impression I was about to confess so that he would come to see me and I would get a chance to argue things out once again. I conceived a plan to hire a private investigator to check the Bangkok banks in case Simon or Alan Soon had deposited large amounts of money. I worked out schemes to get even with James. I contemplated trying to persuade somebody at the Embassy to do some unofficial spying for me. I begged Mother to point out to David Allin the advantages of uncovering information that would lead to my release: "Tell him it will make him a world-famous investigative reporter overnight," I wrote.

I plotted and counterplotted. At night I lay on my bed and wove ever more complicated webs of intrigue. Always at the back of my mind was the fear that the decision I had made—to continue with my not guilty plea and refuse to appeal against my sentence—might have been a terrible mistake. I flung myself into speculation and the composition of agitated letters. My inner turmoil was made worse by the scarcity of information and the frequency with which rumors changed. One week I was told that David Allin was in Hong Kong and had found Simon Lo in prison; the next, it turned out David had not been to Hong Kong at all.

As the time drew near for my final court appearance when I would hear the verdict, I nerved myself for the end of one fight and the start of another—the end of the court processes and the launching of what

I hoped would be an international campaign for my freedom. I felt I had been abandoned by God, by so-called friends, and by justice itself. I was more than ready to cast myself in the role of the martyr at the center of a world crusade. I hoped the world would oblige.

14 Martha

*Please rest easy, Mother, the hard
part is over.*

Letter to Mother, October 13, 1977

On December 9 I was to go to court to be sentenced.

When my name was called, I was surprised; it was
earlier than usual. I wasn't expecting visitors to be
allowed in until later. I wondered if it was the two
missionaries, Margaret and Lucille. I wasn't sure if I
wanted any visitors at all.

Apart from one person, the visitors' enclosure
was empty. I could see the litter and dirt blowing
around her feet. Empty, the room looked grimy and
depressing.

My visitor was an old lady, frail and snowy-
haired, dressed neatly and prettily. She leaned

against the barrier and looked straight into my eyes. She was accompanied by an English missionary who introduced himself as Jim. The old lady spoke with a broad Lancashire accent.

"I'm Martha Livesey. I've just come to see you, love, because I'm from Blackburn, too."

I looked back at her and burst into tears. I saw her giving a bag of food to a guard for me, and then the other visitors came in and the clamor began. I stood at the barrier, clutching it, crying my eyes out. Through my tears I saw her looking disconcerted and trying to make herself heard above the shouted greetings. Though I couldn't hear her, I could read sympathy in her face. I could only sob helplessly, "I want to go home. . . . I want to go home. . . ."

I wasn't capable of saying anything else, and she couldn't make herself heard, so after a few minutes she left. I made my way back inside and numbly took the bag she'd brought me from the guard. Still crying, I went to the kitchen. Several people were preparing food. They looked up as I came in and banged the bag down on the table.

"What's up?" asked Hannah in surprise.

I couldn't explain. I didn't know the words. That woman was from Blackburn. She'd be going to see my mother when she got back there. . . . Suddenly, as if a dam had broken its banks, everything came flooding back: that there was a Blackburn, that it was all still there after my nine months in prison, that there was a world outside where people had names like *Livesey* and lived in Blackburn. I'd never forgotten these things, but the old lady had brought them to my mind with a terrible clarity. She had been so sweet and frail, stepping in from another world into the dirt of the prison.

"I had a visitor . . . from Blackburn . . . an old lady," I sobbed. "I can't stand it anymore, Hannah. I want to go home. I really do. I've spent nine months in this Godforsaken hole, and I want out, Hannah. I want to leave. It wasn't my heroin and nobody will believe me. . . . Oh, Hannah, . . ."

"Don't give me that old innocent victim stuff again!" Hannah knew my tantrums. "We don't want to hear it. We've all got our problems here, you know."

Something exploded in me. I swore at Hannah and the others. I shouted obscenities at the top of my voice. As I stormed out, I grabbed at the bag I'd brought in, intending to take some fruit. Instead I found a booklet which had been put inside. I stuffed it in the pocket of my jeans. I was desperate to get away, to be on my own, to try to sort my head out and think things through.

When somebody was crying in the prison, a crowd soon gathered to jeer or out of simple curiosity. There were no official places for prisoners to be on their own. Even the toilets in Lard Yao were doorless. I knew of only one place where some privacy could be found. Underneath the hospital building, which, like the other huts, stood on stilts, was a dark shady place avoided by everybody because in the daytime, snakes came in from the bushes to find shelter from the heat. I didn't care.

I sat in the cool darkness. The music on the loudspeakers was drowned by the sound of my own pulse in my ears. My heart was pounding. I gulped lungfuls of air in between retching sobs. I was shaking all over. Huge questions battered my brain. Why? Why had it all happened? Why was I in prison? Why did my mother and family have to suffer? I hated being hurt myself, but knowing they were being hurt, too, was even worse. Why? Why? Why?

Memories of the past eighteen months came back to me, each with the same burning question mark hanging over them. Why hadn't I been happy in Hong Kong? Why did James single me out to deceive and lie to? Why didn't I realize what was going on? Why was I the one who had to go through all that hell?

I put my hand in my pocket, looking for a tissue. I pulled out Martha Livesey's booklet. It was a small pocket-sized pamphlet. The cover gave the author and title: it was by somebody called Robert Laidlaw, and it was called *The Reason Why*.

I began to read. As I read, it seemed as if every word in the booklet had been written with me in mind. Had I been the victim of my own foolishness and the wickedness of others? But, I read, that is exactly the problem of the world. Everybody is selfish; nobody ever does good things by nature. Was I angry at God and bitter toward him? Yes, said the booklet; that is what people in the world are like, if they do not know who God really is. In simple language the author explained that there is a thing that the Bible calls sin, that sin makes it impossible for people to have any kind of relationship with God because he is perfect and holy, and that we are all born with it.

As I read on, I realized what sin was. I suddenly

saw, as I'd never seen before, my selfishness and hardness. I remembered my marriage. I'd always acknowledged that there were faults on both sides, but now I remembered specific things I'd done and said, and I was ashamed. I thought of the Kokusai, of times when I'd proudly thought of myself as sophisticated and clever when, in fact, I was being cruel and heartless. More and more things came into my mind, episodes I'd tried to forget. *Sin* was an old-fashioned word, but I knew what it meant, all right.

Sin was the reason why the world was in a mess, why my life was in a mess, and the reason why God had done something about it.

For—I discovered as I read on, absorbed—God had indeed done something about it. He had sent his own Son into this messed-up world, to suffer in it and live among the selfish human race and finally even to die for it. By coming back to life, he had destroyed death.

Suddenly there was an explanation for everything, a reason for my unhappiness in Hong Kong when I knew something was missing from my life, but not what it was; the reason for my restlessness and searching. God had been missing in my life. I saw now that what I had been looking for was something that only he could bring me: forgiveness, peace, love. All my searching for love had led me nowhere. But God was telling me now that there was real love—his love—that made sense of all human loving.

I'd been taught it all before in Sunday school but hadn't understood it. I knew the right words. I could even string together an intelligent conversation with the Martins, but it was only empty words. All the time while I'd prided myself on being a good, decent person born in a Christian country, I'd been keeping God out of my life. But he wasn't going to be kept out. Apparently he wasn't the sort of God you turn your back on so easily. He had come after me. He had even come into Lard Yao prison to find me here under this hospital hut. And he wanted something from me. He wanted my life, he wanted to put it right.

I felt a surge of shame. I had suffered and been degraded and disgraced, but so had Jesus Christ; he, too, had been taken to trial and publicly punished. But unlike Jesus, I was hard and selfish. I had lived my life for my own satisfaction; he had lost his life to save people from their sins. I had given nothing, done nothing, in return. But God had given his Son for me.

I couldn't remember when I'd last prayed seriously. But now I felt an urgency to talk to God, to respond to the amazing things I had read in the booklet. I closed my eyes.

"God. . . ."

I hesitated. Who was I, to be talking to God?

Then the words spilled out. "I'm sorry for the mess I've made of my life. I'm sorry I've not wanted you. Please come into my life and change it. I want to give it to you. . . ."

Again, I hesitated. Here I was, giving my life to God, but what was the gift worth? Probably a life spent in prison for the next few decades, a life spoiled and disgraced. What sort of a life was that, to be giving to God?

And then, deep inside came the certainty: *I made you. I know you. Give me your life, and I will change it. I want you for myself. I love you.*

I must have sat there for ages. Eventually I emerged from under the hospital hut and went inside it. I sat down in the waiting area and gazed out across the compound, blinking in the suddenly bright sunlight. *It's not just us who are in prison,* I suddenly thought. *The whole world's in prison, and I've just been shown the way out. I've been in prison all my life.*

On the far side was the Warden's office. I could see her standing at the window, looking at me. Hannah appeared from the office doorway and came across the grass. The Warden must have sent her to find out what was going on.

"You all right?" Hannah sounded placid and unalarmed. She was used to my moods.

As I looked at her, I could see past her to the prisoners in the factory buildings. The loudspeakers were relaying a march; a rhythmical clash of cymbals and a drone of wind instruments. A guard was leaning against the doorway of the nearest building, reading a newspaper. The smell of the sewer was strong in the sultry heat. From the gatehouse block an odor of fish wafted across; there must have been a delivery.

Hannah raised her voice. "Come on, Rita. Let's get back to work. Maybe I shouldn't have shouted at you. I can see you're upset. OK, so I should have kept my mouth. . . ."

I broke in gently. "It's all right now. It's really all right. Really. All of it."

"Huh?"

"I've just understood something that's been staring me in the face for my whole life."

"You're cracking up. Come on. There's enough to do in the kitchen. . . ." She turned to lead the way.

"I've become a Christian. I finally realized, you see, about God, about Jesus, how it all fits together. . . ."

"Hah!" grunted Hannah and strode off, lost for words.

Later that day I went to the prison library and borrowed a Bible. I began reading it that evening in the dormitory. I had no idea where I was supposed to start, so I opened it at the beginning, at the Book of Genesis. The others saw me reading but didn't comment. I read a few chapters. I remembered the creation story from Sunday school. Now it was different. The God who had made the world—who had put the sun and the moon in the sky and all the rest of it—was the same God whom I had met that afternoon. I didn't understand much about Genesis and had to stop reading because I lost track. But I closed the Bible, feeling happy. I might not know much about God, but now I knew who he was.

I was ready for sleep. I prayed again. I talked to God silently, nothing fancy, just telling him about things that had happened and pouring out some of my fears and doubts. I didn't know what the correct way to pray was. I didn't know if I should be kneeling or putting my hands together or what. It didn't matter. As I talked I knew God was listening. I knew I didn't have to go into long explanations about things, that he knew perfectly well what the situation was. And as I told him everything that was trapped inside me, things that I had never been able to tell anybody before, the loneliness I'd been experiencing disappeared.

As I fell asleep, a last recollection from the day

came briefly into my mind. It was of Hannah, looking at me perplexedly in the hospital hut. I remembered what she'd said: "You're cracking up." I shut the memory out. Whatever had happened in the hut had been real. God had done something amazing. I knew things were going to be different from then on.

Over the next few days I was troubled by frequent doubts. Had I really only been clutching at straws? Hannah made it clear what she thought, in a kind enough way.

"I'm not denying it's important to you, Rita. I don't doubt that it's made a difference. But don't bank on it lasting. I've seen too many girls get religion in this place. It's wonderful for a while. But you're in here longer than a while. It takes a pretty good religion to see you through a place like this."

I spread my hands. "I can't argue, Hannah. I don't know enough about it. But I know it's real. I'm not fooling myself."

Hannah shook her head pensively. "I don't want you to crash any harder than you need, that's all."

Afterward, struggling through the middle chapters of Genesis and trying to make sense of unpronounceable Hebrew names, I thought of what she'd said. Was I settling for an emotional trip, something to blot out the harsh realities of prison life?

But I held on to the conviction that if what God had said was the truth, then it could be tested and checked out. As I prayed, I saw things happening. I saw myself changing. I found that I saw things differently. People I'd taken for granted suddenly became important to me. I was grateful for kindnesses I'd previously ignored. I was learning to love people. In many little ways I was changing. There was no mistaking it; my life was beginning to turn around. God's promise to me that day under the hut was actually coming true.

My doubts often returned, but when I considered what was happening in my life, the doubts lost their power. It wasn't simple heavenly-mindedness, burying my head in the sand like an ostrich. This was something so real, so exciting, and unlike anything I had ever come across in my life before, that— incredibly—it might even have been worth coming to Lard Yao to find it.

I became very concerned about my family. One of the worst things about my being in prison was wondering what the effect would be on them. It was easier for me; I had regular visits from officials and lawyers; my family had to make do with what they could pick up from Embassy letters, occasional telephone calls, and reports from people who'd been in Bangkok and had come to see me. My mother's visit had left her grieving for me, and the effect of my imprisonment on her was one of the things I hated most about Lard Yao.

So, as soon as I could after I had become a Christian, I put Robert Laidlaw's booklet into an envelope and sent it to her. At the back of it was a page headed "Decision," with a place for the reader to sign his name if he wanted to become a Christian. Now my name was written on the page, and I was so sure that Mother would see things as clearly as I had that I had no doubt she would automatically sign alongside my name.

It didn't happen like that. I was frustrated, and pleaded with God. "It's so easy for you," I prayed.

"Please make her see. She needs you just as much as I do. Please, God, do something special."

As time went by, Christians I got into correspondence with went to see Mother and reported some good conversations. But I was so impatient. I wrote enthusiastic letters to her, and she replied carefully, obviously distressed that she couldn't commit herself to something that meant so much to me. "I do pray, Rita. And what I pray for is that God will bring you home." It was as if that was the condition which had to be met before she would commit herself. I could understand why she felt that way. A month ago, I would have felt exactly the same.

15 Sentenced

Today, at around 11:00 A.M., I got a
twenty-year prison sentence. It didn't
come as a shock, but it certainly came
as a surprise. I was expecting over
thirty. . . .

Prison diary, December 9, 1977

December, the month I had been dreading for so
long, found me quite a different person. I had no
way of knowing what was going to happen. I knew
that all attempts to track down Simon Lo had
failed, and I realized that there would be no affi-
davits from Hong Kong to support my innocence.
Mr. Puttri was preparing me for a severe sentence,
and Mr. Lyman was talking about appeals and
amnesties, which assumed I was going to get thirty

years or more. After the months of hard work by my lawyers, the Embassy officials, and people in other countries, everybody had settled down gloomily to expect the worst.

Yet I had the most incredible feeling of peace. It wasn't that I floated around Lard Yao with a seraphic smile. Neither was it a torpid lack of interest in my fate. I cared very much about my future, and I still lost my temper and grumbled and criticized. What was different was the fact that I knew God was in control. When I found myself becoming angry and selfish, I was aware of him helping me. I'd never experienced anything like it. It was as if somebody was standing by my side all the time, and when storms threatened, he tugged my sleeve and drew me back. Suddenly all the "religious" phrases made sense: "The Lord is my Shepherd," "Jesus is in my heart," and so on. I'd heard them and laughed at them before, but now I knew what people who talked like that were talking about.

It didn't matter what the outcome of my trial might be. My life was God's now and he was quite capable of doing what he wanted with it. When I remembered this, it made me see the forthcoming sentencing differently.

"Please, God," I asked, "give me the strength not to despair. Don't let me be bitter. I'm not strong enough on my own." It was a prayer I had to pray often as the tension built up, but he answered it.

December 5 is a national holiday in Thailand, celebrating the King's birthday. Most of the capital is decorated with pictures of the King, colored lights, and flags everywhere. In the prison the holiday was preceded by elaborate preparations by staff and prisoners. Marchers drilled, dancers practiced, and decorations appeared on all prominent parts of the buildings.

The general excitement was heightened by the fact that the royal birthday is traditionally the time of the royal amnesty, when reductions in sentence ranging from a third to a half are given. It would mean that more than three hundred prisoners would be released. The music blared even louder on the loudspeakers, making reading and even sleeping impossible. It was announced that the music was a special treat for us because it was the King's birthday.

"It looks very pleasant, Miss Nightingale," said the English visitor. I'd seen him strolling around with the Warden earlier. "The grass is trim, the paths well kept. I'm going to be able to take a good report back."

He was right. The grounds did look particularly attractive. Prisoners had been set to work tidying and trimming for days in preparation for his arrival.

"Now then." He looked around cautiously. The guard was standing stony-faced at the door. She didn't appear to be taking much interest. "I shall be reporting back when I get to England. You know, I've some influence in certain quarters. What I'm saying," he said, leaning forward intently, "is that I can drop a word or two in the right ears. Tell me, are you happy with the way things are going? What about Mrs. Castle? Do you think she has helped your case? And what do you think the King will do? Will he intervene?"

I recognized the gambit. Lately a variety of people

had visited me in prison, taking an unusual interest in my welfare. There had been a few like him around, trying to trick me into making wild statements and hopefully embarrassing both the Thai and the British governments.

"No," I replied sweetly. "I wouldn't expect the King to intervene. I'm grateful to everybody who has helped."

Not long after, an open invitation was issued to the world press to visit the prison, to see for themselves what conditions were like. Again, the prisoners were detailed to get the place into good shape. We became used to seeing small groups of journalists touring the factories. I had to fend off several who wanted to interview me. My reputation as a troublemaker had increased with the press coverage of my case, and I was very unpopular with the Warden and her guards. It was also the beginning of my rift with Hannah, who bitterly resented the influx of visitors and the fuss that my case was arousing.

At home, the Bishop of Blackburn wrote to the Foreign Office on my behalf, a number of fund-raising schemes were started by the same people who had collected 20,000 signatures on a petition for my release, and I had letters of encouragement and a few Christmas cards. By now I was resigned to not being released. I began to feel that Christmas in prison might not be such a bad experience after all.

The night before I was due to go for sentencing, one of the Thai girls in the dormitory approached me hesitantly. She had something in her hand.

"*Khor thot* (Excuse me)," she said. "I made it for you."

It was a crocheted necklace, beautifully made of

black thread. Many Thai prisoners made such chains to wear instead of jewelry. The Thai people are famous for their skill in handicrafts, and I had admired the patient skill of the girls in the dormitory. I took the necklace gratefully.

"Busaba, it's lovely. Thank you."

She pressed her palms together in the traditional Thai salutation. "I wish you great luck tomorrow, Rita."

"Thank you. . . . Look, I'll show you. . . ."

I rummaged in my box of possessions. Somebody not long ago had sent me a tiny silver-plated cross taped to a letter. I found it and fixed it to the chain. "I'll wear it with the cross tomorrow. It's lovely."

The ninth began like every other day when the doors were unlocked at 6:00 A. M. By seven-thirty all those due to attend court were lined up by the gate. After roll call we were all searched. Often prisoners going to court smuggled letters out for other prisoners, and the guards were looking for these. Then we were crammed into the visitors' enclosure. We waited in the breezeless heat for an hour. Finally, after another roll call, we were herded onto the prison bus.

At the courthouse we were put in the Holding Room. It was windowless, about forty feet by thirty, and contained four rickety benches and the usual toilet area. In my several visits to court, I had learned its nickname—the Hatbox. It was the filthiest room I have ever seen. The toilet stank, and a cracked pipe from the one upstairs periodically leaked into the room, frequently onto some unsuspecting girl who had the bad luck to be standing underneath. Once I was in that room for eleven hours with seventy girls.

Unless people came to visit you there, you were given neither food nor drink. On a previous visit I bribed a guard to get me an iced coffee by promising to make her a cake back in prison. Fortunately, on the day I went for sentencing I was called into the court after only half an hour in the Hatbox.

I was astonished at the number of people in the courtroom, far more than for a normal hearing. A tall Englishman shook hands. "Hello, Rita," he said. "I'm Jim Biddulph of BBC." I saw television cameras nearby. As we talked, bright lights shone on us and the cameras whirred. I was shaken. My mental preparation for this ordeal hadn't included the idea of a full-scale television interview. I began to realize to what degree the press had become interested in my case. I can't remember what I said in the interview except for my reply to his question, "What do you think will happen to you today?"

"I don't believe they'll let me out," I asserted. "They're going to sentence me to imprisonment."

Afterward I sat with Mr. Puttri on the bench that had been assigned to us. Behind were a number of spectators. Among them were Mr. Lyman and Leonie.

I was grateful for Mr. Puttri's presence. He of all people had never tried to raise my hopes, but he was sympathetic and explained matters to me. Mr. Lyman had tried to enthuse me and make me excited about my chances, but by that time I only wanted to be done with the courts and find out the worst. Mr. Puttri was realistic and I appreciated that.

As I sat down, Mr. Puttri looked at me directly. "They are probably going to give you life, Rita."

I knew what that meant in Thailand: 100 years.

"If we are lucky," he added morosely, "we will get fifty years."

There was nothing to say. I stared ahead.

A hush fell over the room. The cameramen drew back; the conversation subsided to a murmur. Everybody stood. Judge Udom Tuchinda and his two colleagues entered and took their seats. The court business began. An official rose to his feet and began reading out a lengthy document in Thai.

I closed my eyes. I tried to think of home, family, anything but the Central Criminal Court, Bangkok. The pictures refused to come. My mind was a blank. Suddenly, without conscious thought, I began to repeat under my breath, "The Lord is my shepherd, I shall not want. . . . Even though I walk through the valley of the shadow of death, I fear no evil. . . ."

It wasn't something I recited following some notion of what a Christian should do at such a time. I hadn't had time to memorize any Bible passages; I'd only been reading it seriously for a matter of days. The words of Psalm 23 had come to me from childhood, from the past, from home; I remembered that I'd learned them as a child. With a thrill of excitement I realized that God was reassuring me. All those years ago, he had known that this was going to happen and had planted his words in my mind. I only grasped this fleetingly; my mind was too numb to think about it, but it was enough. I knew God was with me.

Finally the judges were standing up, collecting their papers. The hubbub of conversation rose again. Mr. Puttri turned to me and permitted himself a smile. "Twenty," he said. He seemed relieved. I raised my head and looked around the room. Leonie left her seat and came to hug me.

My initial reaction was one of tremendous relief. Twenty! Not thirty, not forty, not fifty—but twenty! Why, with remission for good conduct. . . .

Then anger gripped me. I began to weep. "Why only twenty?" I demanded. Leonie looked perplexed.

"Rita, it's wonderful news. We were expecting. . . ."

"They gave me twenty because they know they're in the wrong. . . . It's a stupid sentence. Nobody gets twenty for heroin. It should have been at least twenty-five. Don't you see? It proves I'm innocent. I'm innocent, and they've admitted it. . . ."

Leonie held me in her arms and let me cry. I sobbed out to her and to the newsmen standing around us, "It wasn't me, it wasn't me. . . . They just took away twenty years of my life, and it wasn't me. . . ."

The horror of the sentence swept over me. The prospect of returning to Lard Yao for one day, let alone twenty years, was sickeningly, frighteningly vivid. The guards, perhaps reading my thoughts, moved closer. One grasped my arm. Leonie pushed her away roughly. "Just give her a minute, give her a *minute.*"

Then all of a sudden the realization of what had happened to me under the hospital hut flooded over me. Into my mind, unbidden, came the thoughts, *It doesn't matter. Whatever happens to you now, you've given your life to Jesus. He'll always be with you. You won't be going back there on your own.*

I wiped my streaked cheeks and squared my shoulders. I looked at Mr. Lyman. I could hardly meet his eyes, he looked so sad. I realized that it wasn't just a defeat for him as a lawyer. He genuinely cared for me. He swallowed and grinned at me determinedly.. "We'll appeal, li'l honey."

The peace that had descended on me was the only thing that could get me back into that Holding Room. The judges had left, the court was emptying, and I was taken back to the Hatbox to be greeted by cries of "What did you get?" and "How many?" When I said "Twenty," there were cries of amazement. "*Chock dee!* (You're lucky!)" came from all sides.

Back in the prison, I was distraught from the tension of the day and the knowledge of my sentence. I agreed with those who told me that twenty years was less than we had expected. But twenty years was twenty years, and the guards had already begun to hint that remission for good conduct was unlikely for a notorious troublemaker like me.

I began to realize the implications of the sentence. Instead of traveling the world and having a good time, I would be a prisoner in a foreign country for twenty years. I would be over forty when I was released. I would have become middle-aged in prison. My friends would have forgotten me. My uncles and aunts would be old or dead when I came out. I might even die in prison myself, far away from friends and relatives.

It was impossible to come to terms with the thoughts that now assaulted me. Things I'd pushed out of my mind, because of hopes that I might still be found not guilty, now returned to dominate my thoughts. I found myself contemplating the worst possibility of all: that one day I would open a letter and read that my mother had died thousands of miles away in Blackburn. When I thought about it, I broke down and cried.

Yet it was not long before that wonderful peace flooded my heart again. Even the damp, drizzly weather that followed my court appearance couldn't dampen it. The day after, Hannah had a visit from Gladys Martin, the missionary. Various problems in the prison had interrupted the Martins' monthly sessions inside the prison, and Gladys, who kept an eye on Hannah's son and reported about his progress to her, had to follow the normal procedure for visitors. Even so, Hannah managed to pull strings as usual and secured the lawyers' room. The meeting lasted much longer than the regulation ten minutes.

Gladys asked for me to come, too, as she had read about my sentence in the newspapers. It was Hannah's meeting, and I hardly knew Gladys, so I didn't feel free to talk about my new-found faith. Gladys was the first Christian I had seen since I'd become one myself. I promised myself that soon I'd make sure I had some time with Jack and Gladys on my own.

"Nightingale to the gatehouse block!"

It was my day for visitors. I wondered who mine might be.

As I entered the enclosure, I saw Margaret and Lucille among the visitors. Lucille saw me first. "Rita, we read in the newspapers about your sentence. . . . We're so sorry."

I found it impossible to look serious. I was bubbling inside. They looked at my face in astonishment. Then Margaret, awed, said, "Rita, you're not angry anymore. Something's happened."

I nodded happily. "You remember you were telling me that God loves me? And about Jesus—I just couldn't see it? Well, . . . I can see it now."

A look of delight spread across their faces. They looked at me and they looked at each other and for a while we could only laugh and jump up and down. If the barrier hadn't been there, we would have been hugging each other, but we let off steam anyway, to the amusement of the people nearby.

When we calmed down, Lucille said, "Rita, can we pray together?"

"Oh, yes!"

So, separated by that seven-foot gap, we prayed. Margaret and Lucille both prayed aloud, shouting so that I could hear over the uproar of all the other conversations going on around us. They thanked God that he had shown me the truth; they asked him to help me as I entered this new stage of prison; and they prayed for my family. It was the first prayer meeting I'd ever been part of. When they finished, I said, "Amen," with a full heart.

It was very hard for me to see them go and then to return to my daily routine. I half-expected the reality of my new faith to fade as Hannah had said it would; not that I doubted that God's promises were true ones, but I didn't see how he could make much of a change in Lard Yao. I gradually discovered that, on the contrary, he was changing *me*.

One problem I'd battled with was nightmares and sleepless nights. It happened regularly enough to make me worried; in Lard Yao, sleep was important. You needed all your reserves, and the cumulative depression caused by several bad nights could take a week to disappear. I would often wake up to find one of the Thai prisoners, anxious that my soul had strayed into danger on some dream expedition, shaking me. "Where is your spirit walking?" they would say. One morning, I woke up with swollen eyelids.

"What do you think's the problem?" I asked Hannah. "My eyes look awfully funny."

"I'm not surprised," Hannah replied dryly. "Apparently you kept the dormitory awake half the night. I've never heard you so bad. You were sobbing like your heart would break. Do you have to let yourself go like that? There's others need to sleep. . . ."

"You mean I was crying last night?"

"Oh, come on, Rita. You know you were."

But I didn't know. As far as I was concerned, I had slept soundly. I didn't even remember dreaming. As I slept, God had enabled my mind to be at peace and let my body handle my sadness on its own.

Canon Taylor, the Bishop of Bangkok, visited the prison regularly. He was a very friendly man who made it his business to introduce himself to all the foreign prisoners and also had good relationships with the Thai people in Lard Yao. He once mentioned, his eyes twinkling, that he saw me as one of his "parishioners." He arrived on one of his regular visits shortly after I had become a Christian, and I told him about it.

Before Christmas I went through a time of depression. Of course separation from my family was especially poignant at that time of year. I was also being closely watched by the guards. Now that I was no longer "on trial" and was a full-fledged prisoner, their attitude toward me changed. A rumor that I was about to commit suicide reached the Warden's ears, and she ordered a special watch to be kept on my movements. One day I was standing near the gatehouse block when a guard shouted out to her colleagues, "Get her further inside! She has got twenty years—she might try to run away!"

All this emphasized that fact that I was a prisoner, answerable to others and watched from morning to night. It was amazing, however, how God seemed to know exactly how much I could stand; when I had had enough and couldn't take anymore, mail began to arrive for me—piles of letters and Christmas cards. Many of those who wrote said they were praying for me. My spirits rose. I'd always known I could depend on my family's support, but here were hundreds of people I'd never met who were concerned for me. God answered their prayers. I still became depressed, but it was as if God was waiting at the end of every tunnel to comfort me.

"The choir's arrived!"

Jenny's head appeared around the kitchen door. "Canon Taylor's here. He's come for the service. Wow, I do feel Christmassy!"

It was Christmas Eve, and pouring down rain. Christmas is not widely observed in Thailand except among the foreign population, but we were allowed to celebrate it in Lard Yao. We were well into our festivities. The Thai prisoners and the guards looked on in amusement as we prepared a Western Christmas with all the trimmings. A member of the Embassy staff arrived a few days before Christmas with a chicken, salads, mince pies, and fresh cream. Other goodies arrived from friends. We had almonds, jellies, fruit, coffee, biscuits, jam, chocolate. . . . It all looked quite strange in such a hot climate, but was nonetheless welcome. Leonie had sent in a Christmas pudding and a jar of mincemeat that day. Six of us were making mince pies: a Chinese girl called Lily, Georgina from Canada, Chris and Jenny, Hannah and myself. The final touch of festivity was provided by my forty-two Christmas cards, which we displayed in the kitchen.

"Merry Christmas!"

Canon Taylor appeared at the door, soaking wet, a flurry of wet umbrella and handshakes all around. He twirled his umbrella merrily. "And how is everybody today?"

"Mind where you're splashing!" warned Hannah, and took it from him. He beamed at her.

He had come with the Christ Church choir to hold a carol service. It was lovely. Georgina, Chris, Jenny, and Hannah didn't want to go to the service, so I went with Lily and really enjoyed it. The service ended with communion—my first as a Christian. A Catholic priest spoke to the Thai prisoners and also chatted to Maria in Spanish.

I was very weepy. I was missing my family, and uncertain as to what the future held. That afternoon I started a letter to Mother, in which I warned her that the Embassy had told me that my hopes of a successful appeal might be affected by the amount of press publicity there had been. "It's not going to be easy and I don't know what it's going to do to me," I wrote, "but I have strong faith now, and also I have you and the family."

At 4:00 P.M. an announcement was given over the loudspeaker: "Everybody must report outside their huts for a roll call." Amidst loud groans we all obeyed. After three separate roll calls it emerged that somebody was missing and the guards thought she had escaped. While I was washing later, a call went out for everybody to report to her own dormitory to be counted. Apparently the roll call had revealed that we had two prisoners more than the official count, and the guards were panicking. It got sorted out eventually. A typical ending to the day, I thought. Merry Christmas.

We had a hilarious evening in the dormitory. Maria had a wonderful sense of humor when she chose to use it, and it was good to unwind. I stretched out on my bed, feeling pleasantly drowsy. I reached for my diary and wrote: "Well, it's Christmas. Today has been better compared with the last few, and for that I know I must thank the Lord, because now I know he's helping me. And this peaceful feeling could only have come through him, so who says prayers aren't answered? Not all prayers, it's true, otherwise I wouldn't be here, but who am I to question his reason for me being here, although I think I know why. . . ."

I woke early. It was a gray, drizzly morning. I lay under my mosquito net and listened to the rain. The net was a fairly recent acquisition. I'd paid a small fortune for it, but it was bliss to be free of the mosquitoes.

Under the net was a lovely surprise—a parcel from Lily. I didn't open it then, because I wanted to save it for later. I went to the kitchen to start work, though I doubted whether much work would be done that day.

Sitting with Hannah when I arrived was an official whose presence put a damper on things. The others arrived. Lily had to ice a coffee cake. We busied ourselves in small tasks until eventually the official left.

We hugged and kissed each other. We exchanged little gifts. I was given makeup, a T-shirt, soap— much appreciated luxuries. After coffee and cake I changed into a lovely new dress my mother had sent. I even put my shoes on. They felt awkward after months of my going barefoot or sandaled. We sat around the radio and listened to Christmas carols. Chris and Jenny wept. As the familiar strains of "Silent Night" echoed around that unlikely setting, I busied myself making the fruit salad, glad of an excuse to conceal the lump in my throat.

A power cut put an end to the carols. We had Christmas dinner early, at 11:00 A.M.: roast chicken with stuffing, mashed potatoes, greens—a traditional Christmas feast. Officials were coming and going all morning, staring at the food. In the end we sat down to a cold meal because so many guards had been inspecting the oven and the fridge, making excuses to hover. After the meal nobody spoke very much. We all fell silent—too silent; I knew where I was, and it wasn't in Lard Yao.

We baked nothing for sale in the prison shop that day. In the afternoon we had mince pies and cream. I was feeling so peaceful I even offered a mince pie to my least favorite guard, an enormously fat woman who had watched over me in court.

That night I continued my letter to Mother. It was the hardest part of the whole Christmas for me. I could vividly picture them at home, sitting around the television, Uncle George playing with the kiddies. "I am with them," I wrote in my diary. "Oh, Lord, how I'm with them—letters just aren't enough. . . ."

I wrote to the Embassy, thanking them for the food. I wrote out a well-loved poem:

*And I shall flee from the darkness, from the
    cold place of silence;
for my heart wants flowers to hold in my hand.
Beautiful songs, beautiful flowers. . . .*

I allowed myself to think briefly of all that had happened in the year that had passed. I contemplated the future. *God could burst open the doors of this prison,* I thought, *and I could walk free tonight. I wonder if he will. . . .*

I reached for my diary and added a final sentence: "I've kept it at bay all day, but what a desolate loneliness I feel inside. Will it pass?"

16 Growing

*Terrible letter I wrote you and Ann
last week, but I'm pleased to say, I'm
back on top again. Not all my own
doing, the Lord Jesus has helped me
and I know he will continue to do so,
so I ask you only not to worry about
me, OK? . . . It'll be Christmas when
you get this. . . . I want you to have a
good time, Mother, and please don't
worry so much. I'm reading my Bible
a lot and keeping very much to
myself. I've found a quiet peace of
mind and I'm not thinking about the
future in any way. . . .*

Letter home, December 18, 1977

Incredibly, I woke up on Boxing Day [December 26] with that deep sense of peace. It had to strengthen me through some setbacks. I heard that I had to return to court the next day.

My decision to appeal my sentence had been a difficult one to take, because previously I had decided against doing so. Mr. Lyman, however, advised me very strongly after my sentencing that I should appeal.

"You've got fifteen days to sign an appeal affidavit," he explained. "Don't you think you ought to try every possible avenue of release? How are you going to explain to your family that you had the opportunity of registering an appeal but didn't?"

I thought about it. "Perhaps you're right," I said.

"I surely am right," he declared. "And another thing. If you don't appeal, it's going to look as if you think you got off lightly, and that will make the Official Prosecutor think again." I realized the force of his advice and took it. The affidavit was submitted within the time limit.

The Official Prosecutor has the option in Thai law of appealing against a judge's sentence if he considers it too light. The summons to court which I received on December 26 could only mean that he had lodged a counter appeal. Such turned out to be the case. He was appealing for an increase to thirty years; his argument was that I had clearly intended to distribute and sell the heroin.

Mr. Lyman responded characteristically. "His appeal is a reaction to our appeal for a reduced sentence," he told the press. "It is tit for tat. I personally do not think that he has a cat in hell's chance of pulling it off."

Though it was normal procedure, Mr. Lyman thought it strange that the Prosecutor had appealed. A large body of public opinion supported me; there was even some support for me in Thailand. One thing the Prosecutor's action did achieve: it made me determined to go ahead with my own appeal. Mr. Lyman was optimistic about its chances.

So, all things considered, 1978 began on a high note. If all went well, I would be home before another Christmas.

Another foreigner, Jenny, arrived. Her pliant personality made her particularly ill suited to adapt to prison life. Her arrest had been almost identical to mine; she had been found in possession of three kilos of heroin at the airport. She was Dutch, and became friendly with Chris. Jenny thought she was German at first, because she heard her speaking the language fluently. It was an odd relationship; in many ways they were quite different.

Jenny was an avid reader, for instance, and would devour any reading matter; Chris read nothing but romantic novelettes, which she preferred in English because she found reading Dutch difficult. Their stormy friendship was punctuated by frequent arguments and torrents of flowery Dutch, rising to a crescendo of screams and usually ending in blows. Chris was so big and strong that none of the guards dared to interfere, so I was usually the one who tried to separate them.

Jenny's case was typical of the arbitrariness I saw in prison. Her case was virtually identical to mine, and moreover she pleaded guilty. She was expecting a light sentence, and we all thought she would get one. When she returned after being sentenced, her face was white.

"How was it?" we asked her.

Jenny's reply was a faint whisper. "Thirty years."

The news was met with disbelief. "It can't be right. You've made a mistake. . . ."

"It should have been sixty," whispered Jenny. "They halved it to thirty because I pleaded guilty."

That night Jenny broke down, and was hysterical for several hours. When she finally slept, we discussed her sentence. Nobody could work out what subtlety of law had determined that sentence, when the normal sentence one might expect would be forty, maybe fifty years.

The next day was Jenny's twenty-fourth birthday.

I was sitting in the dormitory reading my new Bible. It was a present from Lucille and Margaret, and I was reading it with the help of some Bible reading notes that Gwen Abbott had sent me from England.

Gwen was a Christian who had seen me on the television news and couldn't forget me. She seemed to hear a voice inside her insisting, "Write to that girl." She'd never had an experience like that before, and wasn't sure what to do about it. After some weeks of the insistent demand, she struck a bargain with God. "Tell me her address in Bangkok and I will write to her!" The next day the newspapers printed the address of Lard Yao. She wrote to me regularly and every time she sat down to write she prayed that what she said in the letter would be helpful. God answered her prayers, because her letters were just what I needed. She also sent me helpful booklets and devotional material such as Selwyn Hughes's *Every Day with Jesus.*

I looked across at Maria. I'd been praying for her for some time. I felt very fond of her, partly because she reminded me of my mother, and I couldn't forget that she had a family outside as well. She was a very religious woman, but also a very sad one, and I wanted her to know the joy I'd found. The problem was, I still didn't speak much Spanish, and her English was very poor. I was helping her with it each evening, but the results were slow.

As I sat watching her reciting her rosary, I racked my brains to think of a way I could share my Bible reading with her. Suddenly, I hit on an idea. I went to Maria's bed and pointed to a Spanish Bible that she owned. I indicated mine and placed the two side by side. Then I showed her the passage I'd been reading in my English Bible. Maria caught the idea. Leafing through her own Bible, she found the same passage. She read it and clapped her hands. "Good! Good! We read together."

We began to spend time together each evening, sharing with each other Bible verses which we found helpful. It was extraordinary how much we could share with so few words. It was also a very frustrating way of learning, which we both found agonizingly slow. Of course I couldn't explain the verses to her—only show her where they were in the Bible— and I couldn't lend her the material Gwen had sent because it was in English.

In the end I wrote to Gwen, explaining that Maria was a Spanish Roman Catholic and asking if she had any booklets in Spanish. "Please send anything you can get hold of," I requested. She did. Soon Maria had Christian literature to read as well as her Bible.

It was hard to accept the sight of a woman in her forties lying on the floor, sharing our rough lifestyle, and bathing with a crowd of others in the morning and evening. We younger women could put up with it; Maria was different. I felt very sorry for her. After a while I could understand her mixture of languages and enjoyed her company even more. She had a sharp sense of humor, and was quite a character as well. At night she would build what she called her "parapets" around her bed, to keep the mice away. She would stuff an old bolster with clothes and odds and ends, and carefully position it around her. Not until it was settled to her satisfaction could she settle down to sleep.

One of the unexpected bonuses of my new "sentenced" status in prison was better sleeping quarters. Hannah arranged for me to share her room, which had only eight other girls in it. I asked if Maria could be moved over from the "on trial" room as well. This was because she was still unable to speak much Thai, and I was one of the very few who could have any sort of conversation with her. The Warden gave permission.

The new quarters were much more pleasant. We were no longer shut up at six o'clock, because some of us were late getting back from our work. My status in the kitchen changed, too; I was now officially working there. Before, I had worked there from choice. Once again Hannah's influence made sure things worked out as we wanted them to.

Sitting up in the evenings was a new experience.

Sometimes I would sit with Hannah and one or two others in the kitchen, listening to cassettes on her player. Often, too, I would sit with Maria in the twilight outside our door, laughing and chatting until bedtime. The others used to laugh at me.

"What are you doing talking to that crazy woman? She's mad—doesn't understand a thing anyone says to her!"

"That's the very reason we should spend time with her," I retorted, but they only laughed.

I was a young and inexperienced Christian. My initial sense of peace was still very strong, but as I prayed and read the Bible, I began to understand that God was doing much more for me than simply calming my anger. He had forgiven me. I had been proud of the fact that I was wrongly arrested, that though others in the prison deserved to be there, I didn't. But as I found out more about Jesus and saw his life in contrast to mine, I became increasingly aware of the things that needed sorting out.

As I talked to him, God made me realize my selfishness, my pride, and many other things I had to face up to. I might have been wrongly arrested for one wrongdoing, but there were many other things I had done for which I had never been punished. And as I realized that, I asked God to forgive me, and he did.

I had always been moved by the plight of my fellow prisoners, many of whom were in prison for some act of stupidity or anger, and had been abandoned by their relatives. I wished I could speak Thai more fluently so that I could talk to some of them in detail; I was very glad that the Martins were around, because they were able to help the Thai prisoners. I developed a deep concern for prisoners in general, not just those in Lard Yao, but all over the world. Sometimes I would lie awake thinking of the hundreds of thousands of people in prisons near and far. One old lady had brought me a booklet; a few missionaries visited regularly, but it was a handful of people, and there were so many that needed to know what Jesus had done for them. I began to pray for prisoners, those I knew in Lard Yao, and those all over the world whom I didn't know anything about personally.

My Christian life was unusual already. My friendship with Maria was the nearest thing I had to Christian fellowship on a day-to-day basis—and we could hardly speak each other's language! A great many things which new Christians learn quickly and relatively painlessly were hard for me to learn, because I was in prison.

I took many of these problems to Jack and Gladys Martin. I had always had a congenial relationship with them; I'd even been to their meetings. But I'd brushed aside their friendly conversation-starters, assuring them that yes, of course I was a Christian, thank you very much. But now I really was a Christian! Their work was mainly with the Thai prisoners, and at the meetings Jack showed films in Thai and talked to them. The Martins had quite a shock when, as soon as the ban on their work was lifted and the monthly meetings resumed, I turned up with my Bible, anxious to learn as much as I could. They were thrilled; they hugged me, and when I tried to apologize for any indifference in the past, they brushed my apologies aside. "We've been praying so hard for you," they said.

They came only once a month, but I saved up my questions, and they sat down with me and helped me. They were the only Christians who ever had regular close contact with me at normal speech levels. Margaret Cole was once allowed into the prison to see me in the lawyers' room, but Lucille only ever saw me through the bars and across the seven-foot gap.

Lucille's faithfulness was something which taught me many things about what the Christian life involves; in her love for me I saw reflected the love of Christ. She was not young, did not have much money, and was not in the best of health. Yet she came to see me regularly, making the tedious journey from Bangkok and often waiting for up to two hours to see me for ten minutes. When Margaret eventually left Thailand, Lucille continued to come on her own.

Lucille put up with frustrating difficulties to make her weekly visit. When I was forbidden visitors for various reasons, she would still wait patiently for two hours or more just so that she could leave a gift for me. She brought me food, various necessities, and Christian books. I would have hesitated to ask my own mother to do what Lucille did for me while I was in prison. Indeed, the other prisoners referred to her as my "mother." "Hey, Rita! Your mother's here!" was a familiar cry on Thursdays. Lucille did in fact write to my own mother regularly; her airmail letters were often brief, but always contained exactly the information my mother wanted.

When I was unable to write because of a mail embargo, Lucille wrote and reassured her.

"Please, Lucille," I urged her after a particularly rowdy visiting session, "don't come every Thursday. I can't bear to think of you waiting for so long, only to end up having to shout like this. It isn't worth it."

She shook her head. "Rita, it is worth it. It's worth it to come here and remember what you used to be like. That makes it really worth it."

If opportunities to spend time with other Christians were scarce, church worship was nonexistent. Canon Taylor, together with a Catholic priest who spoke Thai, held a monthly communion service in the prison. I attended many of those services, and the Easter and Christmas services were highlights, too.

So, though Christian fellowship was nonexistent in the sense that young Christians usually know it, God compensated by providing me with wonderful Christian friends outside the prison and by supplying the answers to my most important queries.

My attempts at Bible reading were a case in point. I was fortunate to have a *Good News Bible*, a modern translation which was much easier to understand than the Authorized Version in the prison library. I began by studying Genesis, but soon ran into problems. I kept wanting somebody to explain things to me. As I read further, I became more and more perplexed, and by the time I was into Exodus, I was ready to give up. Then Gwen Abbott's letters began, and I used the devotional booklets she sent.

I still had problems, however. One day I talked them over with Jack and Gladys.

"I want to read the Bible properly," I explained.

"I'm enjoying reading a little piece every night, but I want to read it right through as well, like any other book."

"Great!" said Jack. "What's the problem?"

"Genesis," I replied gloomily. "I can't make head or tail of a lot of it. I tried jumping ahead to Leviticus—that was even worse."

"Do you know how the Bible is made up?"

"Not really. I know that the Old Testament comes before the New and that's about it."

"It's a collection of books, Rita, written at different times. There are history books, poetry books, letters, lawbooks, hymnbooks—all collected into one volume. They're all part of God's true word to us, but you don't have to start at page one and read all the way through to the end. Would you read a hymnbook right through like that?"

"No, of course not!" I was much relieved.

Jack and Gladys suggested I start with one of the Gospels, and that's what I did. I loved to read about Jesus's life, the things he did and said. As I read about his death and resurrection, the wonderful knowledge that the old story was true thrilled me. He had really died and been raised to life, and now I knew him and could talk to him.

One of the most exciting things about being a Christian was the way the time-worn "religious" phrases became real and meaningful. I was "saved," I was "born again," I had "asked Jesus into my heart." I'd smiled at such things when I heard people say them in the past, but now I knew what they meant.

I had no commentaries or Bible dictionaries. When I came across something I didn't understand,

I made a note of it. If it was a minor problem, I asked Lucille or Margaret before she left Thailand or saved it up for Jack and Gladys if it was complicated and needed an extended chat. My Bible reading really got under way when Jack gave me an American Bible study correspondence course. I worked at it every night, and Jack collected my papers each month and marked them for me. It was very helpful to have to follow a system of study. I was so excited by the Bible that I was always dipping in here and there, finding out what was in the various books. I didn't stop doing that, but it was good discipline to have to read a particular topic as well.

One day when I was in the kitchen working with Jenny and some of the other girls, my mind was busy with what I had been reading.

"Jenny," I asked suddenly, "you know all that about the Ark and the Flood?"

"Huh?"

"You know, the flood that drowned everybody in the world, and God told Noah to build an ark to keep his family safe."

"Oh!" Jenny registered recognition. "It's a story in the Bible. Sure, I know it."

"Well, it's true!"

Jenny raised her eyebrows. "No, Rita, it's a story. It couldn't have happened."

I launched into an animated argument about the flood. The Martins had given me a book on biblical archaeology, and I was fascinated by it. I was fired with the excitement of my new knowledge. Jenny listened patiently, interrupting with an occasional query. At the end she sighed.

"Yeah—I'm really pleased for you, Rita. It's really nice; it's good that you have this thing."

As she turned back to her work, I noticed Hannah frowning at us. She found my new enthusiasm for the Bible irritating and mistrusted it. As my faith grew and didn't wither away, I hoped that she would be sympathetic, but she remained skeptical.

"Oh, people in prison do turn to God; of course they do. They've got nothing else. You were at rock bottom. You saw something you thought you could hold on to. Yes, I can understand."

I tried not to be hurt by such comments, but instead, to think of the things I could see in my life which had changed. I had evidence that Christianity was true. *I* was evidence.

I was sure that anybody who would seriously consider Christianity could not fail to be convinced by it. In fact, I was so sure that I constantly told people about my own experience of God and showed them Bible passages which had meant a lot to me. Mostly they nodded appreciatively and let me finish. I was disappointed that nobody became a Christian upon hearing about what had happened to me, but I found that they gradually accepted that it seemed real and valuable for me at least. Sometimes, when one of the girls was distressed about her case, or was worried about their home and family, I hesitantly suggested, "Would you like me to pray about it?" Often they would say yes. Also as the months passed, some of them began to talk to me about their problems.

I sometimes wondered whether I should be more aggressive about my faith. I read Christian books about people who had helped dozens of people to believe in Jesus. It seemed to be something which every Christian should be trying to do. I was living among Buddhists, atheists, and drug addicts; people were sharing my life who didn't know about Jesus. What should I be doing?

One major barrier to communication was my poor knowledge of Thai. I was able to make small talk with the Thai prisoners, but I couldn't imagine explaining the Bible to them. I just didn't have a large enough vocabulary. So I concentrated on building relationships, trying to put right my earlier dislike and harshness toward them. As I got to know them better, I became very fond of many of them. I shared with them what I could about Jesus, and prayed that God would override any difficulties my inadequate Thai had introduced into the conversation.

Most of the foreign prisoners knew that I was now reading my Bible and praying as well as meeting with the Martins and other Christian visitors. They were amused by the amount of studying I was doing and by the fact that my life was so full. "Why don't you lie on your bed and be bored like everybody else?" I was often asked.

But there was so much to do that I couldn't be bored! Every night I followed the same routine. First I exercised for a quarter of an hour, which was a long time in the sweltering evening heat. I really needed it, and it worked; I kept to the same weight my whole time in prison and stayed in good health. So I put up with the fact that the guards and the other prisoners laughed at me for doing it.

Then I wrote up my diary. My diaries were odd documents—a mixture of my new experiences as a

Christian and the resentments and frustrations with which I was still battling. There were many things which I still had to sort out in my head, and I knew that I must sort them out. I prayed about these things, but it was also a help to write them down in a book which nobody else read. Praying to God was just like talking to a close friend about anything I wanted to. Writing in my diary was helpful in a different way; the act of writing it down helped to release the tension. Even so, as I looked back over entries in my diaries, I could see the change that had taken place. One striking change was in my handwriting. Before, I'd scored the page with the force of my bitterness. Now, my handwriting was clearer, neater, and more even. It was a reflection of the way I'd changed as a person.

I wrote letters next. When anybody in the family had a birthday or an anniversary, I would make a special card, using dried flowers from the prison grounds and bits of colored tissue. I spent hours on little details—lettering and so on. I'd never been a very good artist, but I enjoyed making things. The other girls began to ask me to make cards for them, too.

A large part of the evening I spent reading my Bible and Christian books. I was hungry to find out as much as possible, and the Martins had a knack of producing just the right book at the right time.

I gave Maria help with her English in the evenings, too, and we'd share our Bible verses, pointing them out to each other in our respective Bibles.

Finally, I settled down to sleep. At first, I prayed only in the evenings, telling God what had happened that day, talking to him about problems that I'd had, praying for other people like Maria and Mother and thanking him for the things I'd discovered in that evening's Bible reading. It was a good way to end the day. Later on I began to pray also in the mornings before I got up.

Sometimes I remembered the evenings I'd spent stretched on my bed, cursing my misfortunes and blaming God for abandoning me to Lard Yao. Now I was talking to him, as a Christian! The wonder of the transformation shook me one day when I found myself praying the unthinkable: I was thanking God for allowing me to be imprisoned.

"I would never have found you outside, Lord," I confessed. "I had to come here so you could show yourself to me. Thank you for bringing me to Lard Yao."

I always prayed silently. It was just as well. If any of the others had heard that prayer, they would have thought I was going out of my mind. As it was, I smiled at the irony of the situation and fell asleep.

17 Forgiving

*I do try and I do pray that I will
completely put all my trust in him
and that I accept that however long I
am to be in here is for my good and
it's to fulfil his purpose, because I
know he has a plan for my life. I just
pray for the courage to accept his
will. I'm all talk, because I'm still so
self-centered and proud, and he's
done so much for me.*

Prison diary, March 28, 1978

The beginning of 1978 was dominated by my appeal
for a reduced sentence. Unlike the sentencing procedure, this involved only two appearances at court:
once to register the appeal and then to hear the

result. The first hearing was the one immediately after Christmas, at which I heard that the Official Prosecutor had lodged his appeal to increase the sentence and that the results of both appeals would be given on the same day. I didn't forget that the appeal was being processed, but I was able to put it out of my mind for long periods.

Letters continued to arrive from home. I found one of them very interesting indeed:

"A firm of lawyers in London wants to take up your case. They've asked for all the details. They are international lawyers. They really do sound as though they might be able to do something."

It was an exciting piece of news. The lawyers had offered to assist on humanitarian grounds, without charging any fee or expenses. The head of the firm personally handled a lot of correspondence and paperwork for my mother, who trusted him completely.

The firm strongly advised that we should do everything possible to avoid stirring up any adverse publicity against the authorities in Thailand and that my best interests would lie in using every possibility open to me under the Thai judicial system. In their opinion my best hope of release would ultimately be in securing a King's pardon. I saw this news as confirmation that my appeal had been a wise move.

In Blackburn, an old lady handed over a weekly fifty-pence gift [almost one US dollar] for me at my aunt's shop, as she had done for months. There were hundreds like her in different parts of the world. I was grateful for them all.

The press continued to draw attention to my situation. In February news came that David Allin had been awarded a commendation in the British Press Awards for his work on my story. The *Lancashire Evening Telegraph* pointed out that the paper would continue to reflect the "intense community interest" in my case, and this it certainly did. "I only hope the commendation will attract more attention to the unhappy plight of Rita," commented David, who continued with his three stories a week about me.

It was during a time of very bad tension between me and the Warden that I went to the Martins in great distress.

"I can't stand it."

Jack and Gladys were collecting their belongings together after their monthly visit. Gladys looked up from packing hymnbooks into a carrier bag.

"Whatever's the matter, Rita?"

"It's the Warden. I've tried so hard. I don't know how to forgive her. I don't want to forgive her. She hates me. I know she hates me."

Jack and Gladys sat down. Gladys reached for my hand. "Talk about it, Rita."

"I can't help it; I can't forget all the things she's done to me. She's branded me as a troublemaker, and it's not fair. I'm always getting into trouble."

Gladys held my hand as I released my frustration in a heated tirade. "She wouldn't let me put my arms around my mother. . . . I had to see her in that filthy visitors' enclosure. . . . Oh, I hope somebody does something like that to the Warden sometime in her life. And there was a beating on New Year's Day—

you don't know what it's like in here after you've gone. They're always beating people and it's all the Warden's fault."

Gladys and Jack looked at me thoughtfully. I waited defensively for them to make the obvious comments—both they and I knew that there were things to be said on both sides of the issue. I knew that though I was genuinely trying to relate to the Warden differently, I was still tormented with bouts of resentment and my behavior was still very erratic.

Gladys's reply was quite different from what I had expected.

"You haven't forgiven her yet, Rita."

I gasped. "But you have no idea how much I've prayed. . . . But God hasn't changed her."

"*How* have you prayed, Rita?" interjected Jack.

"What do you mean?"

"You see, there are two ways of praying about a problem like this. You can try to enlist God's sympathy on your side against the other person. Or you can ask God to simply change the whole relationship you have to her. You must choose whether you change or she does."

I fell silent. Into my mind flashed an image of the severe-faced, crisply uniformed woman who ran Lard Yao. I tried to think of her as a friend, as a human being like myself, but I shook my head in despair.

"I can't do it, Jack. I've such bitterness in me."

"That's right. You can't do it. But Jesus can."

Suddenly remembering the changes in my attitudes which I could already recognize, I nodded slowly. Gladys smiled. "It won't happen overnight. You have to go on forgiving. Jesus told his disciples that they should forgive seventy times seven times.

"Keep bringing her to God, Rita. Tell God about your feelings. Don't try to be something you're not. Ask God to change you into what you want to be."

"Satan is trying to make things as difficult for you as possible," added Jack with a smile. "He's letting all this anger build up, until your own bitterness hurts you. You're doing his work for him, Rita."

God followed that conversation up swiftly. Jack and Gladys gave me a book, *The Freedom to Choose*. It was tremendously helpful as I began to put forgiveness into practice. I was finding that forgiving somebody was much more than having warm thoughts about him. It was hard work, an effort of the will. In that hard work the book played an important part. I think I underlined every paragraph in it. What made me particularly happy was that the book dealt with problems which loomed very large in my life and which I hadn't had time to ask the Martins about. God had supplied the answers anyway.

As I learned about forgiveness, my understanding of what was involved expanded, sometimes painfully. Passages in the Gospels seemed to leap from the page and bore into my brain. As I read about the attitude Jesus had toward his enemies, I was ashamed of the state of my heart. I found it hard enough to forgive the Warden, because it meant accepting that I, too, had been in the wrong. But gradually I had to face up to the fact that I had to forgive James, Simon Lo, and Alan Soon as well. I couldn't put the matter out of my mind. God kept reminding me that it needed sorting out. I argued with him as I prayed.

"Why do I have to forgive them, God? They used me. I didn't do anything to deserve it. Surely I don't have to forgive them. They deserve to be punished and humiliated, not forgiven!"

As I fell silent, I was aware of God's answer. He was not going to let me forget. Pictures and memories filled my mind. I saw James proposing marriage to me. I remembered the contemptuous denial by Simon Lo in a hotel room: "Who are you?" An image of Alan Soon, silent and arrogant in the Interpol interrogation, swam before my eyes. Try as I might, I couldn't ignore them. And, as more and more of my deep resentments were brought to light, I had to face up to the fact that I had been nursing bitterness against the police, because they had arrested me and let Lo and Soon go.

It was a slow and painful progression. Each person had to be prayed over, agonized over, and forgiven. When I thought I had really forgiven somebody, I would find myself resenting him two or three days later and having to forgive him all over again.

It was only as I looked back, as the days became weeks and the weeks months, that I saw that my attitudes were changing. I was learning how to forgive.

Still, I had periods of doubt and uncertainty; my Christian visitors had warned me that I would. I never doubted the reality of Jesus, but I often stretched his patience; I demanded the most stupid things, just to test him. He even gave me some of the things I'd asked for.

I was also periodically oppressed with loneliness, when the distance between Bangkok and Blackburn seemed infinite. I feared that somebody would kill me in the prison. There were plenty of assassins inside—convicted murderers who had killed ten or more people for the equivalent of thirty-six dollars each. I was unpopular with some of the guards. Sometimes I would be unable to shake off the fear that one of them had paid an assassin to dispatch me. The fear was, in all probability, irrational. But that didn't make it any less real.

It was especially hard at such times to know that all my Christian friends were outside. Jack and Gladys suggested I pray in the morning before the day began so that I could bring all my worries and fears to Jesus. I began to do so, and it helped.

In all these matters I realized more and more that being a Christian wasn't just believing in a philosophy or a set of religious statements. It wasn't a matter of signing a membership card or joining a church, neither of which I could do anyway. Becoming a Christian was entering a relationship. It was getting to know somebody, and it was getting to know oneself. As I found out more and more about God and what he had done for me, I discovered things about myself I'd never realized. It was this process of discovery, which often involved realizing things I didn't want to realize, that convinced me that Christianity was true.

18 Rejected

*April is the hottest month of the year
here and we're all just about
suffocating at present. . . .*

Letter to Mother, April 23, 1978

"Liar!" said Maria. I gritted my teeth.

"You're imagining it, Maria. It isn't true. They—
are—not—talking—about—you. Do you understand?"

Maria shrank back against the wall. There was a
dubious look in her eyes. "Why they not speak
English, then? Hah! They speak Dutch. Why should
they speak Dutch, if they not talking about me?"
She stamped on the floor, like a judge rapping his
gavel on the bench. She waited for my answer.

"Maria, they are Dutch, you know. Jenny and

Chris are Dutch; that's their nationality. For heaven's sake, Maria, they can surely speak Dutch together and not be talking about you."

Maria scanned the room fretfully. Hannah, Lee, a Chinese girl, and a few Thai prisoners all ignored her. Jenny and Chris stared back at her. She dropped her eyes and muttered angrily.

I was becoming very worried about Maria. She was growing edgy and suspicious. She jumped to conclusions, thinking that anybody chatting quietly in a corner must be discussing her. The episode with Jenny and Chris was the latest in a long line of incidents.

I did what I could to reassure her, but she was becoming more difficult to reassure. *Why do I bother with her moods?* I asked myself sometimes, but then I reminded myself that her case was still uncertain and information was difficult to obtain. She must have been frantic with worry.

She became obsessive about cleanliness. Cleaning the room and wiping it down was one of the prison chores, but Maria went further. Everything had to be just right. I was sleeping between her and a very untidy girl who left books and clothes strewn everywhere. Maria's complaints developed into a vendetta. Often, when matters boiled over into bitter argument, I thought, *This isn't like Maria. She wasn't like this when she first came in.*

The times spent sharing the Bible, learning English, and joking together grew fewer and fewer while her outbursts became more frequent. A minor mishap at mealtime would provoke a fury. I became more worried. I wondered if it was the change of life; there was *something* changing her personality. I prayed for her every day. Maria's friendship had become very important to me, and I was deeply concerned.

People came and went; new prisoners arrived; others left. I found time passing very slowly. Though I had lots to do, I lost the sense of time passing. Sometimes I would leaf through the pages of my diary and think, *I'm sure time passed much more quickly last year.*

Hannah's attitude toward me was changing. She had accepted the fact that I was now a Christian, but she disliked hearing me talk about it. She was extremely skeptical about my appeal. Whenever a fresh burst of publicity blew up about me, she was sarcastic and pessimistic. She felt that I was making a great to-do about something which I should have accepted gracefully; after all, my sentence was only twenty years.

One night in July I was working through an English lesson with Maria when the door of the dormitory was unlocked. A guard began reading out a list of names: mine was among them. "To go to court tomorrow," she explained.

I was frightened. "It's the appeals," I said. "There can't be any other reason. They're going to tell me the results."

Maria put her arm around me. "It'll be all right. Don't worry. It'll be all right. You'll see."

Hannah, across the room, gave a short ironic laugh. "You're in for it now, you silly cow," she called out. "Now you'll get what's coming to you. All this talk and public protests. You'll see where it's all got you now."

I couldn't reply. I lay on my bed and silently

prayed for strength to face whatever was going to happen the next day.

At the courthouse I had to wait several hours before I was called. The Hatbox no longer existed; I was told to wait in another room. I was told afterward by a prisoner that the Hatbox had been removed because of the foreign interest in my case and the journalists who were covering it.

I sat on the floor with the other prisoners awaiting their hearings. I had a book by a Dutch Christian, Corrie ten Boom. I turned the pages and began to read.

At the head of each chapter was a verse from the Bible. Each one of them, as I read it, was like a message from God to me.

I began to pray, my head bowed, as the conversation flowed around me and people shifted around restlessly in the heat. My prayer wasn't hopeless and despairing. I looked around the room and prayed for each of the other prisoners one by one. I prayed for their families, and for their cases. I prayed that God would make himself known to them as he had done to me. Then I prayed for the guards. I told God about the things that were making me resent the guards, and I talked about them with him. As I prayed, I realized that I felt differently now.

I opened my eyes. The Thai girl sitting near me was staring at the floor. *"Sawadee* [Hello]," I ventured. She smiled at me shyly. I asked her what she was coming to court for, and she embarked on a long story only part of which I managed to understand. But it was an opening.

Others nearby saw us talking and joined in. We exchanged simple Thai sentences. They told me

215

about their families; I told them about mine. In other court appearances I had been preoccupied with my own problems. This time God brought me out of myself. I even smiled at the guards as they went back and forth. When my name was finally called, I went quietly. This time I didn't need to be pushed into the courtroom.

Mr. Southworth, the Embassy official from Blackburn, greeted me. Mr. Puttri came over and shook hands.

"Is Mr. Lyman here?" I asked anxiously.

"It was difficult to find out what is happening," said Mr. Puttri. "A messenger has been sent; I think he is on his way."

I sat down with Mr. Puttri. The judge came in. We rose as he entered. When we sat down again, a court official read out a document. This time my Thai was adequate to grasp what it meant. Mr. Puttri confirmed it.

"Your sentence stands, Rita. Our appeal has been rejected."

I felt sick. I hardly registered the fact that the Official Prosecutor's appeal had also been rejected.

Reporters from the Bangkok papers swarmed around, asking questions about prison conditions, lesbianism, and beatings. I ignored them. I was used to trick questions by now. I went over to Mr. Southworth. He looked very dejected. "I don't see how I can have faith in anything now," I wept.

Inside, I knew that nothing would shake my faith in Jesus. My despair was for those who had worked so hard for my release, and now for the impossibility of further court applications.

Mr. Southworth put a hand on my shoulder.

"You have an excellent case. You could appeal higher, to the Supreme Court."

I shook my head. "I had the strongest possible case when I first came into this court, Mr. Southworth. I was innocent. No, I'm done with courts. I will not appeal to the Supreme Court."

Mr. Puttri held an impromptu press conference. "No further appeals," he stated. "The next step is to apply for a King's pardon. This we shall do as soon as possible."

There was a flurried entrance at the door of the court room. Mr. Lyman, breathless and annoyed, entered. "How did it go?" he demanded.

"It was rejected," Mr. Southworth replied. "So was the Official Prosecutor's application."

Mr. Lyman looked at me squarely. "The Supreme Court?"

My face told its own story. Mr. Lyman nodded. "OK, li'l honey, we'll go flat out for a King's pardon."

The guards approached to take me back to prison. "A King's pardon!" repeated Mr. Lyman.

What none of us referred to was the one fact we all knew. In Thai legal history a pardon for a convicted heroin offender was unheard of. Such an amnesty had never been granted.

19 Ann and June

*How can you comfort friends who've
just had such heavy sentences passed
on them? The sentences are getting
heavier. . . . I'm afraid my calm
optimism has taken rather a severe
blow. But don't worry, kid, I'm not
half as upset as I sound. . . .*

Letter to Ann, July 8, 1978

The big event of the summer was the arrival of my
sisters, who came to visit me. Their journey was
paid for by the generosity of the Portia Trust, an
English charity which helps women in trouble and
had interested itself in my case.

"One thing's for certain," I said to Hannah. "There's
not going to be any repeat of what happened with

Mother. I'm going to see the Warden."

"Hope it goes well," she grunted. "You never know your luck."

When Embassy officials made one of their regular visits, I asked if they could also discuss my sisters' visit with the Warden. They said they would do what they could. When Lucille and Margaret came on Thursday, we prayed about the arrangements.

When I asked the Warden if special arrangements could be made for the visit, she agreed that Ann and June could visit me for an hour each weekday, in the office used for Embassy visits. I was thrilled, and very grateful to the Warden.

I was so excited on the day they were due to arrive that I kept jumping up and down like a schoolgirl. At last the loudspeaker blared my name, and I rushed to the Embassy room.

Just as I'd done with Mother, I rushed around the screen and hugged them. They were laden with presents—a lockable cosmetics bag, English tea, my favorite licorice—and some things I'd requested for Maria: cigarettes, some nighties, and other odds and ends. I didn't give the gifts a glance. The sight of my sisters was marvelous.

"You're so grown-up!" I exclaimed over and over. It was true. June had left her school days behind. It made me realize how long it had been since I'd seen them. "And Ann—you've not changed a bit! You look great!"

They were enthusiastic in their turn. "You look so well," said Ann. "And you're so happy," they kept saying. They couldn't get over it. "We've never seen you look like this before. . . . When you came home from Hong Kong, you didn't look like this—it's really from inside. . . . You look marvelous."

"Make sure you tell Mother," I insisted. I would repeat it several times in the week they were in Bangkok. I couldn't forget how I'd looked when she'd seen me in prison, and I wanted to be sure that she would know I'd changed.

"How is Mother?" I demanded. "And Uncle George and Auntie Mary and everybody? What's it like at home? What sort of a trip did you have?" The questions tumbled out.

"She's great," they assured me. "She's keeping busy. We have reporters all over the place now. They keep phoning us. Mother's had the phone number taken out of the directory! We can't go anywhere in Blackburn without being recognized. You wouldn't believe it!" they laughed.

I drank in every detail and studied them carefully. It had been so long since I'd seen them.

"Your skin's so fair," I told them wonderingly. I was amazed at their English complexions. I'd gotten used to seeing dark skin all around me. I was very tanned myself. The prisoners who saw my sisters arrive commented on the same thing. "Your sisters are really pretty! And they have such light skin!"

Each day Lucille took an hour off work to bring them to Lard Yao, and all my friends helped to make them welcome. Jack and Gladys took them sightseeing, so they saw something of Bangkok. I had told my sisters in letters that I was now a Christian, and I was very glad that they were able to meet my Christian friends.

Among the first people I asked my sisters for news of were my Uncle George and Aunt Mary.

Ann and June had been dreading the question. My uncle and aunt had been our next-door neighbors since I'd been born; they were the closest to us after our mother and father. Shortly before Ann and June left for Bangkok, Aunt Mary, who had suffered from arthritis for years, had taken a sudden turn for the worse and had been rushed to the hospital. Within days her liver and kidneys had failed and she was in a coma. Doctors said that there was no more they could do for her and advised Uncle George to prepare himself for her death.

Ann's husband, John, said that they should tell me she had died. It was inevitable, and it would be better if I heard it from my sisters than from an official. But when they arrived, neither could bring herself to say it.

"How is she?" I asked anxiously. I had already heard she was in the hospital.

Ann looked uneasy. "She's very ill."

"But she's going to get better, isn't she?" I insisted. Ann and June didn't speak. A cold fear seized me. Then I heard myself saying calmly, "Yes, she is going to get better."

That night I prayed with all my heart that if Aunt Mary were to die, it should not be until I returned home. I couldn't bear the thought of her dying without knowing Jesus, and I wanted desperately to have the opportunity to share my experiences with her.

A day or two later, back in Blackburn, my aunt moved in her bed and opened her eyes. "Please, could I have a glass of water?" she asked an astonished nurse.

She made a full recovery.

The week with my sisters was wonderful. We shared all sorts of family gossip and caught up on the things we couldn't put in letters. Ann saved a special surprise for me until the last day.

"I went to the doctor before I left England," she said. "It's been confirmed. The tests are OK. I'm pregnant! I wanted you to be the first to know. I haven't told anybody else yet," she added.

As the idyllic week came to an end and we said good-bye, June was in tears. "Don't cry," I comforted her. "I want you to go home. I don't want you to see me here again, because I'll be seeing you in Blackburn. I want you to tell Mother how happy I am, and I want you to keep her spirits up."

I wasn't crying. I felt peaceful and relaxed. Then, as they disappeared out of sight, through the gate, I turned and went to my room. I pushed open the door and lay down on my bed. *Then* I cried—for a whole morning.

God had arranged the visit perfectly. Not only were the arrangements totally different from those when my mother had visited me, but the timing of the entire visit was very precise. The Warden was helpful and sympathetic; she granted the special favors I asked of her. But only a week or two later, I received the news that a public charity in England had decided to launch a new political party: the Rita Nightingale Party. They felt that public sympathy might secure enough votes for me to be adopted as a candidate for the parliamentary seat recently vacated by Barbara Castle. The theory behind the plan was that the Thai government would never dare to hold a British Member of Parliament prisoner.

It was a foolish scheme, if only because of the

effect it had on me in prison. My reputation as a troublemaker, which I was trying to shake off, was dramatically enhanced. The publicity generated was not all favorable toward me, and it embarrassed Barbara Castle, the British government's representatives currently handling my case, and the Thai government. The *Evening Telegraph* in Blackburn quoted (in translation) a leading article from the principle Thai newspaper, the *Siam Rath*:

> It would be a great historical achievement in the annals of Thai history to have a British MP in Lard Yao jail. . . . If she is elected there must be no thought of paroling her or reducing her sentence under any circumstances—let her stay in prison, in Thailand.

I appreciated that the campaign was undertaken and supported out of sympathy and concern for me, but it was one of several examples of organizations not in a position to see the results of their efforts. The Warden was very angry about the publicity and about the new wave of press coverage it generated. Articles appeared which quoted criticisms I was supposed to have made of the prison. I never said the things they quoted, but the Warden didn't believe that. My relationship with her slumped dramatically. I do not believe that a request for special visiting privileges then would have been successful.

The increased hostility from the guards made life difficult, and it took awhile for life to get back to normal after Ann and June's visit.

My fragile friendship with Hannah broke down completely when the new publicity campaign began.

Things became so fraught with tension that I had to stop working in the prison kitchen. This meant that my privileged food arrangements came to an end, and I had to use the prison shop like everybody else. I was put to work in Factory No. 1, where I operated a buttonhole machine. We made children's clothes and sometimes army uniforms. It was hard work when there was a big army contract to fulfil; I went to sleep at night with my fingers rough and aching. When things were slack, however, we were allowed Saturday and Sunday off. A radio played constant Thai music as we worked. Occasionally I persuaded the guard to tune to a Western station playing music I liked. The result was usually a very tearful Rita Nightingale, wallowing in some sentimental ballad from home, until the other prisoners decided that enough was enough.

Now that I was no longer in the kitchen where most of the foreign prisoners worked, I had less opportunity to speak English. I had to buckle down and learn Thai properly. I helped one girl to read the letters she received from her English boyfriend (they married eventually and set up home in Birmingham, England).

Even so I often thought I would never understand the Thai people. I no longer called them animals and fools. I found that like me they had their strong points and weak points. I discovered I had been wrong in many of the judgments I had passed in my bitterness before I'd become a Christian. But I was still perplexed by many of the differences between Thai and Western attitudes.

The factory was built of cement blocks, with a wirecovered gap near the ceiling. Often, birds would find a way in and fly around for a while until they could escape again. One day I was removing some stitching when a small feathery bundle dropped to my hand. A bird had flown inside and blundered into one of the newly installed electric fans. Now it lay in my hand, breathing rapidly, a fatal gash in its skull.

I looked down at it and watched it struggling in its death throes. Suddenly one of the older Thai women rushed over, took the bird from me, and cradled it in her hands as its life ebbed away.

"What was all that about?" I asked one of the English-speaking Thai girls.

She smiled gently. "She did not want the bird to die in the embrace of a foreign spirit," she said softly.

I knew little about Buddhist attitudes to the spirits of animals and birds or about their belief in reincarnation, and I found the incident perplexing. My perplexity increased when a week or two later a girl received a serious head wound from one of the fans while cleaning it. Nobody paid any attention. I was the only one who even reacted. I took her to the prison hospital, and she had to go to an outside casualty department in Bangkok to have the wound properly stitched.

20   Valerie

Maria never speaks a word to me.
She never said, "Good morning," let
alone, "Happy birthday," on Friday.

Letter to Mother, October 17, 1978

I was becoming more and more worried about
Maria. The mystery over her sentence did not clear
up. The brief radio announcement that she'd been
given life was never followed by any official mention of the matter, and she wasn't called to court.

Her behavior became increasingly strange. She
had been cheerful when my sisters were visiting.
That time, in fact, was one of the best I ever had with
her; every day after they left I sought her out to
share the delicacies they'd brought and tell her all
the things they'd said. That was how close we'd

grown. I didn't relate in this way to any of the other girls. I really liked her and felt terribly sorry for her. It was so hard for her, not knowing English well. At least the rest of us could argue with our lawyers.

I doubt if Maria had realized, even then, that she had been sentenced to life imprisonment. She was obviously distressed because she had no visitors and because the legal machine seemed to have ground to a standstill. Because of prison regulations then in operation (which said that letters could only go in and out if they were in Thai or English) she had no letters either.

One day I was sitting with Maria, sewing. She was very edgy, picking up bits of thread I'd drop and winding them into tiny skeins. As I watched her, I made a decision.

"Maria, I'm going to write to your son. He should know what's going on. He may be able to help."

Maria looked up in alarm. "No, no; my son is good boy. Don't bother him."

"But he must be told. He'd want to know."

"My son is good boy. Doing many things for me. No write to him." She began arranging the skeins into rows, carefully aligning each one with the next.

I finally managed to extract an address. I wrote a long letter to her son, explaining the situation and pointing out that as we were unable to get information ourselves she needed outside help. The letter was returned two months later. Across the address Maria had given me were scrawled the words "No such address."

I wondered what was going on. Had Maria given me a false address deliberately or had it been a lapse of memory? It was one more disturbing incident.

Finally after many months, Maria's case began to move forward again. The usual process of preliminary hearings began, and eventually she was told she would be going for sentencing. I sat up with her the night before she went to court. She was very distressed. When she came back the next day, she said that nobody had mentioned life imprisonment at all. She had been sentenced to forty years.

We didn't know what was going on. I didn't know whether the original rumors had been true or false. We weren't in a good position to assess the situation.

I tried to cheer her up. When she came back I treated the sentence as good news. That was a bad mistake. Hearing sentence passed had made Maria realize the reality of imprisonment for the first time. And forty years is a very long time.

As a convicted prisoner she was put to work in one of the factories, but before long she began to refuse to work, staying in her room instead. I tried to argue with her.

"You must go to work, Maria. It's not good for you to spend so much time alone."

"I'm all right. Not want to go out," she replied stubbornly.

"I feel like that, many times," I reasoned. "But you are doing it so often."

It was true; sometimes it was good to stay in all day, just so I could be on my own. Every six weeks or so, when things got on top of me, I stayed in just to be alone. But staying in always involved arguing with the guards and being locked in, so it was effectively self-imposed solitary confinement. It wasn't long before Maria was staying in every day.

She stopped going with me to the prison shop; she

stopped wearing shoes; her obsession with cleanliness and tidiness became fanatical. I was going through a difficult time after the Rita Nightingale Party episode, so I found relating to Maria made me even tenser. The other girls were also becoming impatient with her. In addition to her other idiosyncrasies, Maria would start speaking to herself in Spanish when we were settling down for sleep. A torrent of protest invariably greeted this: "Shut up, you silly old bag!"—or worse. Maria, whose grasp of English was adequate for her to realize she was being vilified, only spoke faster and louder. Eventually a guard would appear to find out what the uproar was about. "Hah! It's Maria—that crazy one" was the usual reaction. The guards usually left us to get on with it ourselves.

Further up the corridor was a group of four small cells, making a unit. Two girls from there had been released recently. "Maria," I suggested, "wouldn't you like to move in there? Then there wouldn't be so many people around you."

She looked at me doubtfully. "You, too?"

"Sure," I replied and went to see if Hannah could fix it up with the Warden. Hannah was only too glad to be rid of Maria, and the Warden gave permission when she was approached. "But it must be a permanent move," she stipulated. "You cannot go back and forth. If you go there, you must stay there."

The changes in Maria meant that we were much less close on the spiritual level. I'd really appreciated our Bible reading, and she had been a help to me in many ways. As she became more distressed, I began to pray specifically that I might have a Christian companion inside the prison, somebody who could help me to help Maria and who would pray and read the Bible with me. I had no idea how such a thing could happen. I couldn't pray that a Christian would be imprisoned in Lard Yao—I wouldn't have wished the place on anyone. But I was desperate for Christian fellowship. I knew I wasn't mature enough to help Maria on my own. "Please, Lord Jesus," I prayed, "send somebody to help."

It seemed impossible, unrealistic. And then, when I had almost given up hope, Valerie came.

Valerie was a prisoner. She arrived with two other girls; they had been held in a prison in Northern Thailand and were moved to Lard Yao while they were on trial. I liked tall, cheerful Valerie right away.

"Where are you from?" she asked me.

"I'm from England. I lived in Darwin, then Hong Kong."

"I'm from Adelaide," she said. "Couple of Aussies, we are! OK, Rita, tell me what's what."

I spent some time with her, helping her to settle in, and we became friendly. After a few days it seemed as if we'd known each other for years.

One day we were sitting on the steps of the hut. I was explaining something about prison routine. I realized she was looking at me thoughtfully.

"What is it about you?" she said. "You're different. You walk around this place and you're contented. You've got twenty years. What on earth have you got to be contented about?"

I took a deep breath and launched into my story. "Well, about a year ago—before I was sentenced, in fact—I was really angry and bitter. I'd been set up to take drugs through customs in Bangkok. I got caught, and ended up in prison while the guys who set me up got away scot free."

Valerie nodded. "Yes, . . . it's always happening. You were the fall guy."

"Was I ever! I was told I was going to get fifty years, or life. . . . I thought I'd go out of my mind. And then I had an incredible experience. I found out about Jesus."

Valerie looked up suddenly. I continued. "I'd known about him when I was a kid. I thought I was a Christian. But I found out I wasn't. And I had to sort it out. In the end I told God I was sorry for everything. I became a Christian. . . . Now I feel peaceful inside. I never was before. Even before I was in prison, there was something missing."

There was a brief silence. Valerie's normally humorous face was thoughtful and serious. Prisoners nearby were arguing vociferously about something; the music on the loudspeakers changed to a different march. We sat wrapped in our thoughts.

"I had an experience, too." Valerie spoke slowly, as if choosing each word before she said it. "It was up in the other prison. I was in a cell, and I began thinking about my life."

I didn't say anything. I listened intently as she told me about herself.

"I was married when I lived in Adelaide. One day I just left my husband and took off with a knapsack. I was looking for something; that was why I started to travel. I don't know what I was looking for, but I knew I was looking for something. I read books—about Buddhism, all sorts of things. One of the things I got into was drugs. I thought they might help me. In the end I bought some stuff from a pusher. The pusher turned out to be a police agent."

I groaned sympathetically. It was incredibly bad luck to have been arrested for drugs when you'd never even tried them.

"So I ended up in jail. One day I was in the toilet or something—anyway, there wasn't any privacy. There never is. All the other prisoners were standing around laughing and talking and smoking cigarettes, and suddenly I blew up at them and started swearing. I went berserk. Everyone ran for safety. Anyway, I stayed in the room all day. And I thought and thought about my life, about the foul things I'd done—I don't mean the drugs and the trial, but everything in my life—and I found myself saying, 'Sorry' over and over again. I couldn't stop. I just kept repeating, 'Sorry,' I don't know to whom."

The other girls, said Valerie, hadn't been able to make sense of it at all. Evidently it had been a deep and catastrophic experience for her.

She asked me more about my experiences. I told her how I'd found the Bible was true, that God existed and loved me. We talked until I had to go. I went off to work in the factory. When I returned that evening, Valerie came running to meet me. She had a Bible in her hand. "Look! Look!" she cried. "Look what I've found in the Bible!"

It was the story of Nicodemus. Valerie was beaming with joy. "It's true, Rita! It's true!"

I was overjoyed. We threw our arms around each other, and for a time we stood hugging each other as prisoners pushed past us, stolidly ignoring our cries of delight. Strange things were always going on in prison.

We prayed together. I asked God to give Valerie a deep understanding, to teach her about himself just as he had taught me.

Valerie spent the next morning in the prison library, reading solidly. There were some Christian books there; some were ones I'd been given and had put in the library. She buttonholed anybody within reach, pointing to something that had impressed her, saying "Hey! Look at this amazing thing I found in the Bible!" The other girls groaned: "Oh, no. . . . Now another's gone like that!"

Her arrival was a definite answer to prayer. But though it was wonderful having her in Lard Yao, I didn't want her to get a long sentence. She thought she'd get twelve months, but I tried to encourage her, saying, "No, you'll get less than that." But somebody else with a very similar charge was sentenced to a year around then, so it was a hard time for Valerie.

We spent a great deal of time in discussion. I think she must have read the whole Bible in a couple of weeks. Her mind was razor sharp; she'd read the prophecies of Nostradamus and all sorts of other weird books, so she had a lot of hard questions to find answers to. No Christians were close at hand to whom I could go for help. We were glad to be able to ask Lucille and Margaret or Jack and Gladys about some of the questions. For the rest, I could only tell Valerie what I had learned from my own brief experience as a Christian and my sketchy knowledge of the Bible.

"Perhaps," she said once during a complicated discussion, "God could have been an astronaut."

"He couldn't be!" I protested, quite sure she was

wrong, but not at all sure how to prove it. I made a quick silent prayer for help.

"Well," continued Valerie, "not in the sense he wore a glass helmet and a suit and all that, but still, when you think of all the planets in the universe. . . ."

"I don't think so," I countered, and tried to point out Bible passages which seemed to indicate God wasn't an astronaut.

These debates weren't destructive or bitter. Valerie really wanted to know the answers, and she had a backlog of questions to ask. For me, it was great; I really enjoyed having my mind stretched. And it was exciting to find, as we studied the Bible and prayed together, that though it was uncomfortable to be challenged to think through what one believed, the Bible really was true and did have the answers.

Most of all, I was grateful that God had provided me somebody with whom to share my faith—one to help me help Maria. That was what I'd prayed for; it was what God gave me. Valerie became fond of Maria, too; because of Valerie's concern, she was able to comfort me when I was distressed about Maria.

"I was up all night with her," I sobbed one day as we were reading our Bibles together. "I don't know how to cope. I explained to her that people aren't persecuting her. I spent all night explaining it, and this morning it's made no difference at all. . . . I've had no sleep all night."

As I wept, my gaze fell on the Bible in front of me. It was open at the passage where Jesus promises that where two or three people are gathered in his name, he will be present with them. I showed the passage to Valerie.

"Maria," she said at once.

I nodded. "Yes. Maria."

"We've got to pray for her, Rita."

So we prayed for Maria, that God would give her troubled mind peace and that he would help us as we talked with her and tried to help her.

21   Changing

Still with all that, I'm happy! Yes, sir!
No way will I get down over these
things again. Maria and I are back
friends, although not as close as
before. Valerie, Aussie girl still here,
but probably leaves some time this
week. . . . I really thank God for the
time we've had together.

Letter to Mother, Ann, and June,
November 12, 1978

"She's got a knife!"

A guard ran across to where Valerie and I were
sitting on the steps of our dormitory hut. "Maria's
gone mad up there! She's got a knife!"

The shimmering, hot afternoon seemed suddenly chill. A crowd gathered, as people emerged from the other buildings and girls in pajamas on their way from their baths stopped to see what was going on.

The guard was frightened and angry. "Do something!" she ordered, pointing at me. "You're that crazy woman's friend. You go and talk to her."

Valerie pulled me back. "You *can't*," she said. "Maria will never take it, not from you."

She was right, I realized. Maria thought I was going to murder her anyway. There was no knowing what she would do to me in that state, if she had a knife.

The guard stood over us, waiting. "I'll go up," said Valerie. "But we've got to pray about it, Rita."

That morning, we had shared Jesus's promise that he would be present where "two or three gathered" in his name. Those words came back to me vividly as we sat on the steps and prayed that in some way Valerie would be able to reason with Maria, despite the language problem and Maria's disturbed state of mind. The crowd watched us with interest. Then Valerie went up the steps and into the building.

The minutes passed. I wasn't able to hold back my tears. Prisoners talked animatedly as I sat with my head in my hands, praying and sobbing alternately. I imagined the worst—that Valerie was lying up there wounded. "Do something!" I urged the guard. "She might be in terrible trouble!"

But the guard did nothing. I wondered if I should go up. Then I realized that if there were a tense situation upstairs, my appearance up there might be disastrous. So I waited and continued praying.

I heard Valerie's footsteps clattering down the steps. I looked up: she was radiant. Her excitement was so great that she could hardly speak. The people standing around pressed close. "It's not a knife!" she stammered. "It's a crucifix! And she understood me! She understood every word I said!"

This was a miracle. Maria had never been able to understand Valerie's Australian accent, and when the three of us were talking together, I frequently supplied a "translation" for her. And now, though highly excited and overwrought, Maria had understood Valerie's words and they had calmed her down.

We both went back upstairs, embraced Maria, and kissed her. We told her gently how harmful it was for her to be on her own so much and reassured her that people weren't talking about her behind her back.

"They're bad," she complained fretfully.

"They're not," we insisted. "You mustn't mind them."

"When did you last eat?" asked Valerie. Maria shrugged.

"We'll make you something," we said. We persuaded her to eat a little, though it was difficult for her after having starved herself. For a few days afterward she seemed to be improving.

Valerie and I often talked about Valerie's future. She wanted eventually to go back to her husband. He was still writing to her, and he'd said she would be welcome if she came back. "It's not that I didn't love him," Valerie explained. "I just had to get away, you know? I realize now what I was looking for. I had to come to Lard Yao for the reason you did—to find Jesus."

She had been God's special gift to me, too. My first regular Christian fellowship! What made it such a special relationship was the way we'd become friends. Her experience in the northern prison was unmistakably the work of God, who was beginning to reveal himself to her. I thanked God that he had allowed me to put some of the pieces together for her and to be a friend at the point where she willingly and completely committed herself to Jesus and became a Christian.

She had such a rich personality, with many gifts. She was an accomplished artist—she drew a magical portrait of Maria which caught exactly that undercurrent of madness that ran in her features at that time.

It was a useful talent, too. Valerie's hair was long, and when she had arrived in Lard Yao, it needed attention. We persuaded her to have it cut. We warned her not to expect too much from the prison hairdressers.

"They're not very brilliant," Chris warned her. "Forget what you've heard about the genius of Thai hairdressing. Our lot missed out on it."

"That's OK," Valerie said. "I'll draw what I want." And she drew a beautiful portrait of herself, complete with earrings, the way she wanted to look. Then she went off to the hairdressers.

An hour later we heard her cheerful whistle. When she appeared we gasped in admiration. She looked stunning. Her hair was short, framing her slender strong-boned face and emphasizing her startlingly blue eyes. It was the sort of haircut you would have been happy to have anywhere in the world. We couldn't believe Lard Yao had managed such an amazing feat.

We talked together to some of the other girls about Christianity. Many others listened in to the conversation—in the crowded prison rooms it would have been hard to avoid being overheard! There was one girl in particular who was a friend of Valerie's. When she was about to be released, I gave her a booklet about Jesus, after I wrote inside it, "Hoping that the things you've heard Valerie and me talk about will give you food for thought, if not now then in the future—think about these things. Love, Rita." But her release was unexpectedly delayed, and the booklet I thought she would read out of prison was, in fact, read in prison. When she finally did say good-bye she grasped my hand.

"Rita, that book has given me something to think about. I did listen to a lot of what you and Valerie talked about. But I'm not going to do anything about it now. If I did, people would say it was only a reaction to prison. When I get home, I'll make up my mind about it." So we had somebody else to pray for together.

It was not very long after the incident with the crucifix that we saw, sadly, that Maria was deteriorating again. A blank, strange look had come into her eyes.

One morning we were lining up for our hot water together.

"See—they're doing it again. I see them," muttered Maria.

"Huh?" I responded absently.

Maria pointed at Chris and Jenny. They were talking Dutch. "They talk about me. They are speaking *Dutch*." She looked cunningly at me. "They speak Dutch so I will not know. But I know."

Behind us in the line somebody laughed. "Maria's flipping again."

I lost my temper. "I spent half the night telling you, Maria, people don't talk about you behind your back. But it's just a waste of breath! I'm sick of you saying it. I won't listen to you anymore. I won't, I won't!"

Without a word, Maria seized the pan of near boiling water and flung it at my face. I barely managed to dodge; drops of the scalding liquid spattered my face. Valerie pulled me out of harm's way.

"You can't stay here." She was white-faced. "I'll wait in line for you. She's out of her mind."

I went to find Hannah, who was angry. "I told you," she said. "You go in with a crazy one like that and that's what happens. Didn't I tell you so?"

The result of the episode was that the Warden forbade the guards to allow Maria to stay in her room all day. She wandered around the prison instead, shoeless, dressed in an old sarong. Eventually the authorities took action. She was committed to a mental hospital in Bangkok, and was there for two months.

The day for Valerie to go for sentencing arrived. We prayed together before she went. She was quietly confident. "I feel I'm going to be allowed home, because I've found what I left Australia, my husband, everything for."

She was given a light sentence because of the small quantity of drugs involved and the circumstances of the arrest. They gave her three months and allowed the time already served in prison to be taken into account. She was to be released in a week's time. When I knew she was going out, I gave her some of my prison diaries to take out with her and post home for me. I'd kept the diaries a secret from the prison authorities, and smuggling things out of prison was forbidden. I worried about breaking the rules in this way, but in the end I just couldn't resist seeing the diaries sent safely home.

Lucille and Margaret had prayed with us that when Valerie left, I wouldn't feel it as badly as I expected, that I wouldn't be shattered. It really did happen that way. I was sad when she left, but not devastated. I was happy for her, and I could see that her time for release had come and mine hadn't. I didn't know why the long negotiations for a King's pardon hadn't made any apparent progress yet, but I simply carried on with my various activities and thanked God for giving Valerie to me for as long as he had. I was surprised to find myself reacting like that. I had feared that I would be heartbroken. Observing my peaceful acceptance of Valerie's departure, I took it as one more example of the way God was controlling my life.

In one connection, however, I especially missed her: my relationship with Maria. Valerie and I had prayed together; we'd seen God working in so many ways. But now Valerie was gone, and Maria was in the hospital. What was God doing? Why had he not at least given Maria peace of mind, if for some infinite reason it was right she should stay in prison?

But he hadn't. She was in the hospital, living in some weird mental nightmare, out of my reach and beyond our help. I did not know what would happen. Of all the hard things I had to accept in prison, Maria's suffering was one of the hardest to bear.

1978 drew to a close. I had been a prisoner for nearly two years and a Christian for just over one of them. My case was still regularly discussed in the newspapers. I was visited by various important people who seemed anxious to hear my version of the story; on one or two occasions I was summoned to meet them in the Warden's office, and found silver tea things set out.

One evening, some weeks after Valerie had gone out, I was on my way up to the dormitory when I found my way blocked by a guard.

"Stop!"

She stood in the corridor between me and the room. I stopped.

"Whatever's the matter?" I said innocently. The guard folded her arms.

"You cannot go in."

I scratched my head. I couldn't think of anything I'd done wrong lately. It was hard to take the situation seriously. The guard wasn't one I knew very well, and my rather perplexed smile was meeting with no response.

"Why can't I go in?"

"You being punished." A thin sneer spread across her face. "You in big trouble. You had letter."

By now completely confused, I was about to

demand further information when I saw movement behind her. Two more guards were carrying things out of the dormitory. One had my box of possessions, the other my bedding. They dumped their loads unceremoniously in the corridor and walked past us, not looking at me.

"Those are *my* things. What is going on?"

"Your things are being searched."

I turned my back on her and ran downstairs and out to the kitchen. Hannah was clearing up.

"What on earth's happening up in the dormitory?" I said breathlessly. "All my stuff's been thrown out!"

"And so have you," returned Hannah equably. "You really are in for it now."

"What am I supposed to have done?"

"Don't you know? You gave Valerie your precious diaries to take out. And Valerie wrote you a nice letter telling you all about it. Went into all the details. I expect you'll be able to read it after the Warden's finished with it."

I couldn't believe it. Not Valerie. She had been here; she knew the score; she of all people wouldn't have done such a stupid thing.

But she had. As the reality sank in, I heard my name being called on the loudspeaker.

My interview with the Warden was not pleasant. She was extremely angry.

"You will lose all mail privileges and all visiting privileges for three months after Christmas. You will be moved from your dormitory. Do you understand?"

That night I entered my new dormitory as the most unpopular person in the prison while, amid

244

protests and scowls, I lugged my pile of belongings into a cramped little floor space such as I hadn't seen since I'd become a member of Hannah's privileged entourage.

Yet in spite of the punishment hanging over me, it was a wonderful Christmas. Canon Taylor organized special services with his Roman Catholic colleague (a Thai-speaking American who had made his home in the Bangkok slums in order to be near the people he had come to serve). Jenny and Chris came to the carol service and met a Dutch lady in the choir, and just like the previous year we ended up crying as we sang the carols.

My second Christmas in prison was a much more significant experience than the first. It's true I had been a Christian twelve months before, but then I had been moved more by the familiar traditions and symbols bringing the world of home sharply into my mind than by what those traditions were talking about. A year later, I could look back on God's presence in my life, the reality of Jesus Christ, and the ways in which he had changed me. Christmas was now not simply an age-old festival of well-loved carols and Bible stories. It was a celebration of the birth of Somebody who had become the most important Person in my life.

We received gifts from each other and from visitors. One of the gifts I received was a book of Christmas carols. On Christmas Eve I took it with me to work. The machine I operated in the factory didn't need continuous attention; I propped the book against it, and for the whole day I sang carols at the top of my voice, tunelessly and joyfully. My Thai fellow prisoners must have thought I was crazy. Tears were streaming down my face—tears not of sadness but of joy, because for the first time I was singing the familiar words with a real understanding of their meaning.

On Christmas Day I woke up depressed. The trouble with the Warden dominated my mind. I lay in bed as the others got up, and I relived the episode over and over again. I knew I should not feel bitter toward her. Jack and Gladys had told me that, and I had realized they were right. So I consciously forgave her for her harsh punishment.

But another thought intruded: an unwelcome one. Smuggling things out of prison was against the rules. *It's a silly rule,* I thought fiercely. Part of me responded with an unbidden thought: *But do I, as a Christian, have the freedom to pick and choose which rules in this place I'm going to keep and which I'll break?*

It's an un-Christian rule, I argued with myself. *It's petty and it doesn't make sense.* Again, I heard myself arguing back. *Of course it makes sense. Just because you're not doing something really wicked doesn't mean that others might not be. Do you expect the Warden to trust everybody to do the right thing? This is a prison, for heaven's sake!*

I sighed in frustration. It was a familiar experience. Ever since becoming a Christian, I had been aware of that voice. Before, I had seen myself as fighting a just war against every aspect of the prison. Now I was reluctantly being forced to admit that, for all Lard Yao's severity, depersonalization, and brutality, Rita Nightingale wasn't exactly a model prisoner. The Warden whom I had just so painfully forgiven might have some justice on her side after all.

Lord Jesus, I thought gloomily, *when I asked you to change me, I didn't want you to change me as much as this!*

I got up and joined the line for washing. Afterward, the foreign prisoners headed for Hannah's kitchen, taking the Christmas goodies which had been sent in. Cooking facilities were there as well as Hannah's radio, a source of blessedly Western music. I picked up my own Christmas things, started after them, hesitated, and changed my mind. I went off to the library instead. As I went by the kitchen, I heard somebody saying, "Where's Nightingale off to?"

In the deserted library I sat down and spread out the Christmas cards I'd received. There were fifty. As I looked at them I began to relax. A feeling of contentment flooded over me. *Why do I need to dwell on trouble and friction?* I asked myself. *Look at all these cards. Some of them are from people I've never met!*

I examined them again, one by one: the pictures of holly, the Dickens coach-and-horses outside nostalgically English inns, the funny cards, the solemn ones. I read the messages inside. Some were intimate, loving assurances from members of my family; others were a few words from people I didn't know; still others were from officials and other individuals who were helping me in my case. England and the English Christmas were very near at that moment.

Outside the building the usual prison noise went on and on. It was beginning to be a hot day. I daydreamed for a while and then began talking to God. I took each card and prayed for the person who had sent it. As I prayed and thought about family and friends and home, I realized that God was with me.

It's difficult to describe. It was as if somebody was sitting with me in that room. I felt the way you feel if you are sitting facing away from somebody who is perfectly motionless. You can't see him or hear him, but you are aware of the fact that someone besides yourself is there. It was like that. I knew that Jesus had come to be with me.

I sat for what seemed a very long time, talking to him and thanking him for everything. Eventually I went to the kitchen where the Christmas festivities were in full swing. All told the day went really well; Hannah was in a good mood. We laughed a lot, reminisced about the past year, and hugged each other a great deal.

Christmas was always at heart a sad day in prison. The Thai prisoners didn't celebrate it, though it was a holiday for Western prisoners. At such times, imprisonment was hardest to face. There were many thoughtful faces around, and not a few tears.

But that was a wonderful Christmas. Not because the realities of prison life were any less evident; they weren't. It was wonderful because for the first time I really understood what Christmas was about, and because God had come to me in prison.

22 Anita

*God is watching over it all, so it's not
our place to worry.*

Letter to Mother, Ann and June,
December 28, 1978

1979: a new year. The first of January celebrations
meant special food and other concessions. On New
Year's Eve, I was alone with Jenny. We could hear
rowdiness in the men's prison some distance away.
A passing guard asked us what we were doing.
"We're thinking of all the things we would be doing,
if we weren't here," said Jenny. The guard grinned
and nodded in the direction of the men's prison.
"You're best off where you are."

In the dormitory I scratched two marks in the
floor near my bed—a calendar. There were just over

eighteen years of my sentence left. I tried not to think about it. I worked out the time difference between Thailand and England, and at the right time I imagined the church bells ringing in Blackburn to welcome the new year. *Happy New Year, Mother.*

During the first months of the year, while I was being disciplined over the incident of the diaries, Lucille came to see me each week even though I wasn't allowed visitors. Each week she made the tedious journey out to Lard Yao so that she could leave me food or some other small gift. After a few weeks the officials decided to put a stop to this, so they refused to accept the food for me and left it uncollected, to rot. Even so, Lucille continued to come each Thursday. I could scarcely believe such sacrificial love.

Also during those months Margaret Cole wrote to the King of Thailand. She explained that as a missionary her reason for being in Thailand was to work with impoverished Thai communities. She pleaded with the King to be allowed to serve my sentence herself so that I could go free: "I am an old woman; I am almost at the end of my life. Rita is a young woman. I believe that she has a work to do for God, among prisoners in many prisons." She did not argue that I was innocent, but drew attention to the fact that my life had changed. I do not know whether the King personally read the appeal or whether it was dealt with by a government department; in either event, it was rejected.

When I heard about the letter, I was shattered. I had not known that anybody could contemplate such a thing. I tried to find words to thank her, but she wouldn't listen.

"I would be as happy in there as out here, Rita," she explained.

"I'm as happy as anybody could be in this prison," I insisted gently.

"No, Rita," Margaret said. "I would be happier than you are. I would have the extra happiness of knowing that you were free."

More foreign prisoners were arriving in the prison. Tall, beautiful Anita, a Greek with a model's figure, came in before my disciplining was lifted. She was unbelievably good-looking—thick henna-dyed hair framing classically perfect features. Anita was her nickname; her real name was Diana, and I could never remember her Greek surname. She spoke English perfectly with a faint accent. She was only twenty-two, but looked much older. She had been using heroin since she was fourteen.

Chris and I, who weren't users, had little in common with the prisoners who were. We couldn't sit and talk about our trips and the highs we'd had. Consequently we didn't get to know Anita very well. She became friends with Ilse, a Viennese girl. When Anita went to court, she told them she was an addict, and they gave her one year. She accepted the sentence philosophically. She knew that she hadn't done badly.

People like Anita had no option in prison but to go "cold turkey" to come off heroin. The guards were expert at finding any drugs that were smuggled in. Once, when cigarettes were banned, a quantity of marijuana was brought in by a visitor. Within hours it was confiscated. For this reason Anita didn't relish the thought of a year in Lard Yao.

One evening in February I was sitting on the steps of the dormitory hut in my pajamas, ready for bed.

"Rita."

I looked up quickly at the familiar voice. A forlorn and ill-looking figure was crossing the grass. "Maria!" I cried. We embraced. I was thrilled. She had recognized me.

I held her at arm's length to look at her properly. I gulped. "Maria, your hair! What happened?"

All the hair on one side of her head was gone. Her scalp was scratched and grazed. The remaining hair was wild. Maria's eyes shifted uneasily as I looked. Her shoulders were trembling.

"Is nothing," she said, looking down at the ground, running a hand through what hair was left in an attempt to cover the poor ruined scalp. Later I was told that in the hospital they had had to strap her down; Maria had managed to get one arm free and had clawed at her head until she had made herself bald.

It was not long before the old pattern began to reappear. What improvement there had been lasted for at most a month. The decline that followed was rapid. One day she was coherent and lucid; the next, she was saying that the hospital staff talked about her behind her back.

"No, Maria," I insisted. "It's not true. Stop. Think; this is how you began to get sick last time. Think about yourself, not about other people. . . . Think about God, about your life; talk to me. Don't let yourself be ensnared again."

She listened, and it was obvious that the words were making sense to her. But she couldn't help herself. Before long, she had to go back into the hospital. When she came out again, she was desperately sick in her mind. She didn't recognize me, and she was violent with the guards. She craved the dark and took to staying in the old punishment block, where she lived like a filthy animal. When I visited her there, she would occasionally recognize me; usually she ignored me.

It was heartbreaking to see her deteriorate. Before, she had always been neat and tidy; one of the first signs something was wrong had been the development of this trait into an obsession. But now she lived in her own dirt like an animal. The authorities had done what they could; she had been to the hospital twice, but it had not cured her.

Somebody who took a great deal of interest in Maria's sickness was Anita. Desperate to get out of prison, she thought that anywhere in the world would be preferable to Lard Yao, even a mental hospital where, indeed, it might even be possible to get drugs. When she found out that the authorities had actually sent Maria outside to the hospital, she was very excited and asked numerous questions.

Anita suffered from epileptic fits. The Thai prisoners were terrified when she had them, and Chris was usually summoned to deal with her. It required Chris's strength. Anita was phenomenally powerful during a fit; she once threw me across the room with a single twist of her body. This was not sufficient to merit her being sent to an outside hospital, however; there were medical facilities in the prison. So Anita, whose behavior was always unpredictable and was more so now that she was withdrawing from heroin, devised a way out.

Anita came rushing into her dormitory with her

hair wildly on end. As the other prisoners sat rooted to the spot, she seized a mirror and smashed it on the floor.

"You fool!" I shouted. Anita ignored me. Bending down, she selected a razor-sharp sliver of glass. She stood up. Glaring at everybody, she quickly and expertly slashed her right arm. Blood trickled slowly down.

Two or three girls jumped on her and forced the glass sliver out of her hand. A piece of cloth was ripped into bandages, and somehow or other the wound was dressed. Anita stood passively, breathing heavily, watching the proceedings with contempt. When the bandaging was finished, she left the dormitory without a word.

We followed her to see where she would go. She was walking slowly and deliberately to the Warden's office, her bandaged arm held like a weapon across her body. She went in. We waited breathlessly; later we found out that Anita was demanding to be sent to a mental hospital. The demand was refused.

When she reappeared she was glowering. She marched up to the dormitory again and came out with another sliver of glass. Before we could stop her, she had slashed her other arm. She rushed to the main gate and stood against it. Ripping the dressing from the arm that had been bandaged, she stood with blood pouring from both arms, screaming. The guards stood around her, waiting for a chance to overpower her. In the end it took several of them to drag her to the ground. Her wounds were forcibly stitched. She achieved her wish to be hospitalized; when she came back after six weeks, she was more cheerful and served the rest of her sentence without further incidents.

It was so sad, though. I said good-bye to her on the day she was released. "I hope you'll be all right outside, Anita."

She smiled. "Yes, I think I'll be OK. I should be able to pick up some dope outside the gate."

When the mail ban was lifted, I once again had the support and encouragement of friends who wrote to me from all over the world. I had known only a few of them before my arrest. Some who wrote to me sent prayers and love; others were working for my release in various ways. Through their letters, I came to know them as real friends.

A Liverpool man, Albert Downing, hitchhiked from Melbourne to Bangkok simply to talk to me for ten minutes. His hobby was traveling, and he had been in Australia when he heard of my imprisonment. He also traveled to Lourdes to pray for my release. Blackburn residents sent funds raised through various projects. Little children all over the world wrote to say they had heard of me and wanted to send me a letter. In Adelaide, Australia, a lawyer who had begun writing to me the previous year was organizing numerous funds and functions to support me. Margaret's church in America sent me a cassette recorder (I wasn't allowed to have it in prison, but was very moved by the gift). A Londoner, Frank McManus, wrote me wonderful letters which I looked forward to. There were many others. I valued them all.

In America, a group called Prison Fellowship

began to write to me and send me their newsletter. This was the group founded by Chuck Colson, who had been a special aide to President Nixon, and had been sent to prison for his involvement in Watergate. Colson had become a Christian during the Watergate investigations, and when a prisoner, had felt tremendous concern for those in prison with him. The Fellowship was formed to show the love of Jesus to people inside prison. I was thrilled that such a group existed. It was an answer to all the heart searching I'd had about the plight of prisoners. God was doing something; he had started such a group.

My application for the King's pardon was made during the first part of the year. There were a great many forms to complete. Mr. Lyman was brisk and decisive. "We have the papers here, Rita. Now we have to have them signed. This is the formal application for the King's pardon. We have to do it exactly right."

Mr. Puttri produced the papers from his briefcase. "You sign here . . . and here."

I bent over the forms and signed my name where Mr. Puttri indicated. Mr. Lyman clapped his hands. "Well, that's that. Now there will be more forms for you to sign later; the prison has to authorize the appeal, too."

When I went to the prison offices to sign the next forms, the official dealing with me read out the questions.

"What is the reason for this application?"

Something snapped inside me. "I've had enough," I replied simply. "I shouldn't be here in the first place, and now I've had enough. And I miss my family. I want to go home. That's the reason for this application."

As the official began to translate what I had said into Thai and write it on the form, I left.

I knew that in deciding not to appeal to the Supreme Court and to appeal to the King, I was asking for something unique, so I had been told, in Thai legal history. I did not like to think of my chances of success. The prisoners ridiculed the idea.

My faith in God was growing all the time, but I refused to allow myself to think that the appeal might be successful. Even those closest to me wouldn't commit themselves. I could only wait, for however long it might take.

As summer came and went, the number of foreign prisoners continued to increase. There was a shift in the government's policy, stronger measures were being taken, and more drug offenders were being sent to prison. Most of them were in for comparatively minor offenses and did not get long sentences. I was quite friendly with all the foreign prisoners, although it was always an agony to see them leave; they were going after such a short stay, and I was sentenced to twenty years. But I knew that the future was something that God knew about and so I didn't need to be afraid. If he wanted me to stay in prison for twenty years, he would make those twenty years as fulfilled and significant as the rest of my life. I knew it; I believed it; but all the same, it was hard to see others going out. At such times I still felt very lonely.

Two new prisoners, Mary and Linda, arrived.

They were Americans, stunningly attractive black girls. Mary, in her thirties, was short and very pretty. She had a nice Afro hairstyle when she came in, but let it grow out. Her clothes were lovely. Linda, on the other hand, was tall and well built, a very jolly girl who laughed a lot. On the evening they came in, we talked together in the dormitory.

"Hey," giggled Linda. "Where's the wardrobe?"

She peered around the room comically. I laughed. "There isn't one in this suite, I'm afraid."

"Waal, . . . I'm afraid this is gonna get all creased." She rummaged in the bag she had brought in with her and produced a beautiful evening dress. We were very impressed; the Thai prisoners clustered around and passed it from hand to hand, exclaiming over the quality of the needlework—high praise, because Thais are usually accomplished in that art. Linda rummaged again. "I got these, too, girls. . . . When do we get any dancin' done in this place?" She handed me a pair of expensive high-heeled shoes. These, too, were duly examined by everybody, but Linda was so big that her shoes didn't fit any of us when we tried them on. She rolled her eyes humorously. "I'll keep 'em safe for when we go visitin'," she promised, folding the dress and placing it back in the bag.

"You gonna have to keep that dress safe for a while, then," said Mary. She was combing her hair with a plastic Afro comb. She looked troubled. "Sure hope this business don't go on too long."

"It depends," I volunteered. "The courts move terribly slowly. You have to go through the procedures. . . . Sometimes they pass light sentences."

Mary frowned. "Hope so," she muttered. "I got

six kids out there. Being looked after. Hope they're all right."

She brightened after a while and began laughing with Linda.

To my surprise, they turned up at Jack and Gladys's monthly meeting. In conversation afterward, I discovered that Mary had been brought up as a churchgoer and that Linda was interested in Christianity and wanted to know more about it. As Valerie had been, she was curious to know how I had managed to retain any peace of mind in the prison. We had some good talks after that, and I told her how I had become a Christian. I began to pray for them very specially. The three of us became close friends and spent a lot of time together. It was good to talk again about Christianity with sympathetic friends in prison. Our relationship wasn't as clear-cut as mine had been with Valerie, who had become a Christian in Lard Yao. Mary and Linda were very willing to talk about Christian things, and I didn't probe beyond what they were prepared to discuss. I prayed for them and tried to answer their questions as completely as I could.

Poor Mary found prison life very hard going. Like many extroverted people, she was a sensitive person when you got to know her. She loved reading the Bible, and would often sit pouring over it during her free time. But the obscenities which were part of the general conversation in the dormitories were a great trial to her. She hunched over her Bible, hands over her ears, vainly trying to concentrate while people all around her were talking and shouting and swearing, and occasionally a couple who couldn't restrain their affection for each other began kissing in full view of the outraged Mary.

"It's terrible!" she complained to me. "Those women! They're swearin' and makin' blasphemous jokes and I don't know what else!"

"Yes, I know," I said peaceably.

"But do you know what they're sayin' in there?"

"Of course I know what they're saying—and doing!" I retorted, perhaps more sharply than was necessary. "I've lived here for over two years. I know what goes on. But you're making yourself worse than they are: you're trying to make them change. You can't. But you can change yourself; you can see them as people not monsters." I was especially sorry for Mary because I had had to go through the same adjustment myself.

"But the noise," repeated Mary. "It's plain ridiculous. I can't even read my Bible with all that goin' on."

"Yes," I replied, "I've been through that problem, too. You just have to change your routine, study in the daytime, in the library."

Mary took time to find her feet in prison. I was often frustrated, because I wanted her to make faster progress. She easily became tense, especially when she was worried about her children. But when she did begin to settle down, she became much more peaceful.

Ubol was a high-born Thai of strikingly good looks; she was in prison for check embezzlement. Her English was impeccable. I was chatting with Mary one day when she approached us. "Please, I want you to pray for me. Will you pray?"

I was surprised; it wasn't the sort of request one

expected from Ubol. I looked at her, concerned. "Why, Ubol, what's the matter?"

"I have had a letter from my sister. She says that my husband is planning to take legal custody of our children. If you pray I know it will be all right."

I had prayed aloud with only one person—Valerie. I hadn't done so with anybody since she left. I looked at Mary. Mary, always anxious for her own children, nodded to Ubol, and she sat with us. We held hands. I prayed and so did Mary, and Ubol said a few words.

Afterward we didn't release our hands immediately. Ubol thanked us quietly. "I really think it will be all right now."

Later that morning I hesitantly said to Mary and Linda—I don't know why I felt so embarrassed about it—"Why don't the three of us get together to pray each morning?"

"Oh, Rita!" beamed Mary. "I've been waitin' weeks for you to say just that!"

I felt terrible. I had been thinking of myself as a sort of "older Christian," but I hadn't suggested such a simple thing until then.

We met each morning on the grass behind the hospital hut, before we had to go to work. People picked their way past us; it was like having a prayer meeting in Piccadilly Circus or Times Square! We didn't mind the curious stares or the crowded situation. We had some wonderful times. Our relationship became very close, and we began to be very open with each other. One example of this was the morning when Mary was struggling with her problems. She was agonizing over her children. We'd prayed about the situation, but Mary talked on and on about it. It was as if she wouldn't leave the matter in God's hands—she kept putting it down and then picking it up again. I wondered how to talk to her about it, prayed about it, and in the end decided on a rather aggressive approach.

"Mary, you are so immersed in your own problems—have you even thought of praying for me this morning?"

"What do you mean?"

"Well, I'm waiting for a King's pardon," I said. "I'm waiting to hear whether I'm going out or not."

"Oh, you'll get that," retorted Mary irrepressibly, as if it were the easiest thing in the world. I shook my head.

"It's not that simple. I've been here awhile and I know how easily things go wrong. But it's in God's hands; we can pray about it. But we haven't, have we?"

I wondered whether I should have spoken so strongly, but that morning Mary did pray for me; it was lovely to hear her pray.

A Thai girl who went to Jack and Gladys's meetings was with us that morning, too. When Mary had finished praying, she prayed, "Lord, thank you for what Rita has come to mean to us. Thank you for her pardon."

It took a moment for it to sink in. She was praying about my pardon as though it had already been granted.

Why had I been so slow to suggest that we meet for prayer together? It was something I'd dreamed of when I'd first become a Christian, when I was one of a few foreigners in Lard Yao; so why didn't I?

I don't really know. Why are Christians so shy to

speak to strangers in the street about Jesus? Why are we embarrassed to pray aloud in public?

I don't know. But I wish I'd conquered my shyness sooner. It was such a wonderful thing to be part of that group.

23   Pardoned

Freedom Hope for Drug Girl in Thai Jail
Daily Mail article caption, December 1979

During the eight months or so that it took for my application for a King's pardon to go through the official channels, I never allowed myself to build up any great optimism. I knew that the government of Thailand had been placed in a difficult situation over my case. They were constantly being urged by the West to be uncompromising in their treatment of drug-traffickers, and I had been found guilty in a Thai court of that offense. The publicity generated in the press around the world over my arrest and imprisonment only made it less likely that I would be released. If I were, the government would appear to be weak in enforcing its controls, and there would be no deterrent value in my sentence. There would be a grave risk that the impression would be given to any drug smuggler that the only action needed to secure release was to stir up sufficient publicity.

I knew, too, that the things which I had said in the past—and even more, the things I was wrongly reported to have said—had not increased my chances of an amnesty. The prison authorities often saw statements in the Western press which distorted or falsified things I had said, and there was no way I could mend matters. On top of that, I was hardly Lard Yao's most docile prisoner at the best of times, and in the first months of my imprisonment I had built up a record of disobedience and intransigence which would not easily be forgotten.

It was such a messy situation, seen from my viewpoint. The government had a difficult situation to deal with, but still, I knew I was innocent. The prison authorities had good grounds for complaint about my attitude. On the other hand, like all prisoners, I had seen brutality and discrimination so often in the prison that I wasn't readily going to see the authorities as faultless. In other words, there was no clear argument that I ought or ought not to be freed—except that I was innocent, and that argument had been defeated in the courts.

Even when my lawyers did permit themselves the luxury of cautious optimism or when I heard rumors that my application was receiving favorable consideration, I refused to get excited and did my best to forget the whole thing. I had left it in God's hands; now I had to learn to leave it there.

It was easier to say than to practice. At the back of my mind there was always the thought, *Maybe....*

But I forced myself to keep remembering the other possibility, *Maybe not*. I tried to prepare for the worst, to accept that my life would be lived in prison for the next eighteen years. I honestly tried to think only that God was in control of my life and would make it a wonderful life wherever it was lived.

He encouraged me in countless ways. He sent people to talk to me at the very times I needed them most. He provided me with books and other help when Christians weren't around. When I read the Bible, certain passages seemed to have been written directly to me; I would read them with the same excitement that I read letters from home. I loved St. Paul's letters, many of which had been written in prison; through them God taught me things I could never have learned elsewhere. One day I opened Paul's letter to the Roman church, and read these words:

> We know that in all things God works for good with those who love him, those whom he has called according to his purpose. Romans 8:28.

The words were a special encouragement. Paul had been in prison; he knew how difficult it was to believe that God was working for his good when he was locked up and separated from his friends and family. Yet he was able to write "we *know* . . ."—not "we hope" or "we believe." I accepted the words as God's message for me and thanked him for them.

Another encouragement was the knowledge that by now hundreds of Christians all around the world were praying for me. When Martha Livesey had left Bangkok after visiting me, she had gone on to

Australia, where she received my letter telling her I had become a Christian. From there she went on to America and Canada. Everywhere she went, wherever she addressed meetings, she talked about me and asked people to pray for me. "Prayer chains" were set up, and I heard about them from Gladys and others. Gladys often reminded me that every hour of the day somebody somewhere was praying for me.

The letters kept coming. I wasn't allowed to have them all, because they had to be scanned by the prison censors, who were getting swamped by the quantity of mail I was receiving. Eventually Christians aware of the situation appealed to people to stop writing to me. That appeal might usefully have been listened to by some organizations in the West which mistakenly thought that the best way to get me released was to flood the authorities with letters pleading for my release and sometimes accusing the authorities of injustice. Apart from the obvious deterioration that this brought about in my relationship with the authorities, it created a practical problem by swelling the volume of mail that was arriving.

But even when I wasn't allowed to have the mail to read, I was moved and thankful that so many people were praying for me and writing. Some people wrote to Gladys and Jack, and though they would always strictly observe the prison rules—it would not have crossed their minds to smuggle mail in to me—they did share some of the contents of these letters with me in conversation. (It was very noticeable that God honored their care to follow prison regulations. None of my Christian friends ever broke them. When my mail ban was operating earlier in the year, Lucille never tried to break it, though other prisoners thought I was stupid not to try to persuade her; yet she managed to pick up enough information about me from official sources and the Embassy to be able to write to my mother and keep her in touch, even though I was forbidden to write.)

I did receive one letter which had been through the censor's office; it was on the official writing paper of the Vatican. It was from the Pope's office, and it said that my imprisonment had been brought to his notice and he would be remembering me at Mass.

I was overwhelmed by the kindness people showed me. Somebody regularly sent me the novels of Morris West, which I really enjoyed. I never found out who the sender was—labels and letters often got detached and lost in the censor's office. Baskets from Jacksons of Piccadilly, a first-class London foodstore, arrived at intervals from another friend whose identity was never revealed. In this case I wrote to Jacksons to express my gratitude, but they wrote saying that they didn't know who had ordered them and could not find out without an invoice. So the baskets remained a mystery, like many other gifts I received. I always wrote to thank people for any present which arrived with the sender's name and address attached. However, many well-wishers must have wondered whether I ever received their gifts.

There were many encouragements. But I was worried for Mother. She had to be finding the

uncertainty unbearable. When I wrote to her, I tried
to encourage her to think my way:

> Don't listen to rumors, Mother. Just forget them.
> The people over here don't know what's going
> on, and they often don't know how applications
> are dealt with anyway. . . . We can only pray
> now, Mother. It's all we can do, and it's in his
> hands anyway. . . .

Mr. Lyman gave me what information he could.

"December 5—the King's birthday. That's the big
day; we'll hear then. Now you hang on, Rita. We've
done all the formal application. I heard the other
day that there's a good chance we'll pull it off."

"It's always the same," I said. "Just hints and
possibilities. Nothing certain, ever."

Mr. Lyman looked at me sympathetically through
the grille. "I know, li'l honey. It must be really hard
for you, not knowing. Well, just as soon as we hear
anything, anything at all. . . ."

"Don't worry," I assured him. "I'm not pinning
my hopes on anything. I promise you that."

He tried to cheer me up. "We'll celebrate when
you get out. What we'll do is. . . ."

I cut him off short. "Don't say that!"

He looked hurt. I apologized.

"I'm sorry. But I don't know if or when I'm going
to be released. I might have to go on living here for
another eighteen years. Please don't talk about my
getting out. I'm really trying not to build my hopes
up."

I found it difficult to pray. I would talk to God

about the future, and I would try to talk about a future in Lard Yao, but all the time the possibility of release was distracting me. The prospects of release dimmed and brightened and dimmed again. Though I refused to raise my hopes, I couldn't help seizing on every rumor and wondering what lay behind it.

A Chinese girl, Su, had become very friendly with me, and she became very protective. She understood my confusion and helped me through some bad times. Our prayer meetings continued. Mary and Linda were praying hard for my release. We learned a lot about caring for each other; I found that with others bearing some of the load of my worries I was able to spend time praying with Mary and talking about her children. Hannah, her natural pessimism coloring her view of what was happening, nevertheless tried to be enthusiastic. Most of the other prisoners avoided raising my hopes.

Mr. Coleshill, the British Consul, arrived one day in November. He was very depressed.

"I'm not at all sure things are going well," he said. "Bangkok is full of Western reporters. They're waiting for the King's birthday. It might go against you."

"How?"

"It's the kind of publicity the government would wish to avoid. It could decrease the chances of an amnesty."

I could understand this. Mr. Coleshill said very little about it, but I supposed that with the international implications of releasing a convicted drug smuggler, the Western press might ruin my chances just by what they wrote. Mr. Coleshill would not confirm this. I was impressed by the way he gave me what information was relevant to me but avoided discussing the wider implications. It gave me confidence that the small encouragements he did give me could be relied on. I tried, though rather unsuccessfully, to be detached about the possibility of anything happening on December 5.

When the day came and went without any announcement about me, I was devastated. Mr. Coleshill assured me that the application was still alive. "We'll hear something any day now. . . ."

Something had changed in me. December 5 had been the day when I had been sure that God would do something special. Either he would let me go home, or he would give me the spiritual ability to rejoice in my imprisonment. I had expected wonderful things to happen. I had looked forward, at the very least, to my doubts and fears falling away, and a quiet acceptance filling my heart. That was what had happened in the lives of great Christians I'd read about. Why hadn't it happened to me? *God, I prayed, what's going wrong?*

Christmas was a blur, dominated by my obsession with release. I stopped eating. Su tried to make me eat but I refused. I began to make excuses to avoid praying with people. Worst of all, I stopped praying on my own.

There is a classic symptom of prisoners called "gate fever." I had heard of it; now I knew exactly what it was. I found myself thinking for hours about nothing but the gate. I opened my Bible and saw only dead words. I tried to pray, and as I called out to God, all that was in my mind was that iron gate and the dusty road behind it. I wasn't even thinking of home and family. It was the gate that dominated my waking thoughts and my dreams—the gate, symbolizing all that Lard Yao was and all that prevented me from walking out to freedom.

It was a catastrophic spiritual crisis. I poured it all out to Jack and Gladys. "I can't think, I can't read my Bible, I can't pray. I can't do *anything*," I sobbed. "I know that's wrong. I know God is in control. I just can't help it—I can't get that gate out of my mind. It's not the uncertainty that's the worst thing. It's not being able to talk to God about it."

Then Gladys said something which cut through the fever and went straight to my heart. "Rita, I don't know why I'm saying this—I believe the Lord is saying it through me. Rita, this is your last hurdle. You must let go completely. In prayer, in your heart, you have got to let this fever go."

Her voice held a quiet authority. Nobody knew yet what the outcome of my appeal to the King would be, but I heard her words of assurance and believed them. I didn't know what "your last hurdle" meant, but I knew that God had spoken to me through Gladys.

"I'll try," I promised. My voice was quavering. Like the embers of a dying fire, doubts and questions still thrashed around my brain. That night, I talked to God. I cried so much at first I could hardly form the words, but when I calmed down, I told him everything. Memories of unresolved bitternesses and resentments came to mind. I thought of the Warden, the symbol of prison authority. Had I really forgiven her? More, had I asked God to forgive me for my attitude to her? I talked each problem through.

As I talked, I was aware of God showing me more

and more things that needed to be faced and prayed about. When I finally fell asleep, exhausted, it was as if a burden had been taken from my back. When I woke the next morning, the gate fever was gone; in its place was the peace which I had not experienced for many weeks.

I began to work hard at the Thai language. The prison authorities allowed foreign prisoners time off work once a week in order to learn it. I'd gone along from time to time, more to get away from work than for anything else; I'd picked up a working knowledge of Thai from the other prisoners. But now I got involved enthusiastically. Each week a few of us gathered in the prison library to study.

It was during one of these mid-week study sessions that the door of the library opened and two women came in. One was Gladys Martin; the other was an American. Gladys spotted me and introduced us.

"This is Kathryn Grant."

I liked her at once. She was a missionary on her way back from a visit to Japan. We began chatting, and the other girls joined in. We couldn't work out how the visitors got inside; it wasn't the regular day for missionaries to visit. But they had applied for permission in the normal way and had been granted it. "We were really praying about it back in America," laughed Kathryn. "So many people have tried to get permission to enter the prison to see you, we didn't think we'd much chance, but they let me come in with Gladys!"

"How did you know about me?" I asked.

"It was Prison Fellowship," she said. I recognized the name at once—the group Chuck Colson, the

Watergate ex-prisoner, had started, and which had been corresponding with me. He had given Kathryn a copy of *Life Sentence*, his autobiography, as a present for me. "Chuck knew I could break my journey from Japan and stop over in Thailand. 'Make sure you see Rita,' he said, and here I am!"

I was thrilled. God was breaking wide the prison doors not to let me out, but to let Christians in. *I don't have to go outside to meet him,* I reminded myself contentedly. *He's here inside with me.*

Kathryn talked about Prison Fellowship, the work it was doing and the vision it had for the future. It was wonderful to see in detail how God was reaching out to prisoners all over the world. He had given me a deep concern for prisons ever since I'd become a Christian, and now here he was, showing me in a visible way that he was dealing with the problem.

Before we parted, we prayed together. It was a sober moment. Kathryn was leaving behind somebody with almost eighteen years to serve in prison; I was saying good-bye to someone whom I had suddenly grown fond of. We were both in tears, not hopeless tears, but tears nonetheless, because prison is a place of separation.

Life went on in the familiar routines of prison. The prisoners often told me, "There's no chance of your getting out." But I was able to handle the thought now.

"Nightingale to the gatehouse block!"

The familiar summons echoed around the prison. It was a fortnight or so after Kathryn's visit, but it wasn't my visiting day. I was taken to the Embassy room. Mr. Coleshill, the Consul, was there. The muscles in my stomach tensed into a knot. He had been to see me only yesterday. It must be really bad news if he had come back so soon.

"Is there something wrong?" I cried. "Mother—is she? . . ."

He shook his head and smiled. "Everything's fine," he said. "Come and sit down."

I sat down opposite him. Between us, the metal barrier was solid and permanent. Mr. Coleshill reached his hand forward and pushed his fingers through. "Hold my fingers while I talk, Rita."

I took hold of his hands through the barrier. I had no idea what it was all about. "Let me read you the front page of the *Bangkok Post*," he said. As I clutched his fingers, he read the news of my pardon. I burst into tears.

He read on. One word leaped from the article—*unique*. It was, according to the *Bangkok Post*, a unique pardon. *That's God*, I thought immediately. *It was impossible without him.*

Mr. Coleshill finished reading. He laid the newspaper down. "It was in today's paper," he explained. "We can't find any more information. I've tried to find out what's going on."

The feeling of deflation was like a physical blow. All my excitement drained from me. I looked at him with a dull, blank face.

"It was a hoax. They didn't mean it. It's just a joke."

The Consul shook his head. "No, Rita. It's no joke. You know the Thai people; they're not joking. This is the *Bangkok Post*, Rita. It's true." He took a card from his wallet and pushed it through the bars.

"We've asked for information to be given us as soon as it's available. But that may not be possible. Take care. When you are released, this is the telephone number you must ring."

When I emerged into the prison yard, I was trembling. I began to laugh a huge, violent laughter that was dredged up from deep inside me. I looked up into the blue hazed sky, and I let out a great scream of joy. Then I began to run at top speed, still laughing uncontrollably. Running was not allowed in the prison grounds, but I flew the length of the compound to the building where Chris worked. But she had already seen me; she started running to meet me, and we met halfway. There were no explanations needed. "I knew you'd go out. I knew, I knew!" shouted Chris ecstatically, hugging me in her crushing grip. We wept and laughed and wept again.

"Maria," I said. "I must go and tell Maria." So we went to see Maria, sitting in her dark room alone.

She had been locked in at her own request. I pressed my face to the bars, ignoring the stench, and I wept. I called her name. "Maria! Maria, I'm going out. I'm being released!"

There was no response—nothing. She sat in silence, her face turned away, as if nothing was happening. And that was how I parted from Maria. It was as if all the wonderful things, the Bible readings, the prayers, the miracle that Valerie and I had witnessed, the improvement after her first visit to hospital—it was as if all had never happened. I did not doubt God, but I did not understand what he was doing then. "Maria!" I called again. "Maria!" There was no answer.

Chris gently took my arm and led me away. We went to tell the other girls. The news had already reached them. Most were thrilled. One or two wouldn't meet my eyes. It was too much to handle. I knew how they felt. I'd felt the same when people were released.

The Thai lady who had looked after me burst into tears and hugged me. A girl whom I had often paid to line up for hot water for me came over and hugged me, too. We all talked at once, as the celebration rose in volume.

There was a sudden hush. The Warden had appeared. She stared at us all, tight-lipped; her gaze traveled around the group. When she looked at me, I looked down at the ground, but could not stop laughing. She went away again without a word.

I began to thirst for details. What day was I going out? What would happen? Where would I go? Mr. Lyman had tried to tell me about the procedure for release, but I had always shut him up because I hadn't wanted to raise my hopes. This was different. Now it was official. I went to the Warden's office.

The Deputy Warden was there. I suppressed my simmering excitement and greeted her with the appropriate formality. Vainly trying to appear casual, I remarked, "I've got a pardon. I'm going out!"

"What?"

"I've got a pardon from the King. I'm going out. When am I going? What date has been given?"

She laughed. "No, no. You haven't got a pardon. Not a chance! You won't be released. You have twenty years!"

"I have a pardon, I have!" I insisted. "It was in the newspaper!"

"No, no, no! You haven't got a pardon," she repeated. "Not Nightingale; no pardon."

"Well" I said tightly, "just suppose, for the sake of argument, suppose that I *had* got a pardon, and it was in today's newspaper. When would I go out, if that were the case?"

She went and consulted colleagues. I heard their laughter. Nobody would believe it.

Finally she said, humoring me, "Not before weekend. Impossible. Paperwork. . . ." It was Wednesday. I nodded delightedly. "OK! OK! That's fine by me, just fine! I only wanted to know!"

After that, my appetite disappeared again. Su sat beside me at supper, feeding me tasty delicacies of fish, but I couldn't eat.

That night I sat up talking with the other girls. My mind was a jumble of all sorts of emotions. Jenny, with her thirty-year sentence, sat holding my hand. I fumbled for words. "Jenny. . . ."

"You don't have to say anything. I'm so happy for you." Her sad face belied her words. "You're going out. And I'm here, I'm still here. . . ."

I knew she was happy for me, but my heart ached for her own sadness. I was frightened for her and for others I was leaving behind. We sat up all night, and I held Jenny's hands the whole time.

"I don't know what it will be like outside," I told her. "I'm frightened. I don't know whether there'll be trouble still waiting for me, in Thailand or even in England. But if there's anything I can ever do to help you, Jenny. . . ."

She nodded thoughtfully. "You cared for people, Rita. You were one of the few. And that's why you're going out."

In her own way she was acknowledging God's providence. I would never say that my pardon was God's "reward" for anything. The Bible tells us not to look for rewards, and there are a great many Christians serving him faithfully in dreadful situations from which he hasn't released them. But Jenny recognized that God was supremely involved in my release.

Next day I went with Chris to the prison hospital to arrange for the transfer of a supply of headache pills I had in my name to hers. Afterward we sat on the hospital steps.

"Think of it!" exclaimed Chris. "You'll be on a plane soon!"

I buried my face in my hands. Suddenly everything was too much to cope with. "Don't, Chris," I pleaded. "I can't imagine it. My mind won't go outside these walls."

I went and did some packing. I decided to give the rest of my books to the prison library. I wanted to keep my Bible and some other things. I would give my blanket to an old Thai lady whom I had gotten to know; it was an expensive European one; she'd never seen such a thing before. That was all the sorting out I did then. I believed I had until the weekend. I did no work that day and ate nothing.

I met with our little prayer group, not knowing it was for the last time. They asked me, "What will we do now that you're leaving?"

"You must keep the group going," I replied. "I could have suggested we meet like this months ago, and I didn't. Now that we have started it, it mustn't stop. The best thing you can do for me is to keep praying. It doesn't matter that I'm going. It matters that you're praying together as Christians. You don't even need to pray out loud if you don't want to."

The loudspeaker was calling my name. "Nightingale to the Warden's office," the disembodied Thai voice announced.

I discovered that my knees no longer obeyed me. I couldn't stand up. "Lord," I prayed frantically, "please, just get me to that office." The unknown future, which I'd successfully kept at bay in a flurry of good-byes and packing, was suddenly upon me. Somehow I managed to get to the office.

On the way, a prisoner called to me, "Tell her, Rita! Say what you think of her! You can give it her straight, now—you're leaving anyway!"

I was torn by a mixture of emotions. The old resentments flared up again. "Lord, hold me back," I prayed. But I couldn't help myself; I remembered all the grievances I'd held against her, the anger I'd felt over Mother's visit, the visiting ban, and scores of other things. I was going to leave prison. She would no longer control me. *Now, surely, I can tell her what she's done to me?* There was no answer; I wasn't listening for one. I had become determined to have my last fling.

The Warden was waiting for me with several prison officials. They were shrinking away from her; she was very angry indeed. She glared as I walked in: Rita Nightingale, the most difficult prisoner in Lard Yao, the one who would never be paroled or pardoned—now to be set free.

When I had been at my most rebellious, I had expressed my rebellion most aggressively in my attitude to the Warden. When she had refused to speak to me in English, I had refused to speak to her in Thai. To speak English to the Warden had become a symbol of my antiauthority stand. I had also refused to give her the respect that was usual in the prison. I would not make the deferential bow and press my palms together in the Thai gesture of greeting. While most prisoners, because of the Warden's rank, actually sank to their knees on entering her presence, I had made a point of drawing myself up a couple of extra inches.

Since my conversation with Jack and Gladys about this, I had made a great effort to conform. But she was so much a physical embodiment of the prison and the authority which had imprisoned me that I fought a constant battle with my resentment. I had taken no other problem to God so often as this. But as I entered the office, my awareness of her as a fellow human being was replaced by a sudden and uncontrollable surge of the old bitterness.

I opened my mouth, determined to take maximum advantage of this opportunity to say all the things I'd suppressed over three years.

But before I could get a word out, an extraordinary feeling of peace descended upon me. I hadn't slept, I had been in a state of nervous excitement for many hours, and I had been rushing around doing a hundred things simultaneously. Then my walk across to the office had brought me to a fever pitch of excited resentment. And now it had vanished. In its place was an absence of hate for the Warden. It was more even than that. After three years of bitterness, after months of prayer which I thought had only been partly answered, I had finally come to feel love for this woman for whom Christ had died. As the realization swept over me, I found myself sinking to my knees before her, my hands clasped, my head bowed, in the traditional Thai gesture of respect toward a superior.

"Yes, Warden?"

I hardly noticed that I spoke in Thai, or that she replied in English. She waved a document at me. Her normal icy restraint did not conceal her anger. "Do you know what this is?"

I could not answer.

"It is a pardon from His Majesty the King," she said. "Sign this document."

I had to sign in several places. I didn't know what I was signing. She was trembling. I was still aware of that amazing peace. She gestured angrily. "Now get your things and go."

I ran to the dormitory. Already some of the guards were trying to pack my things for me. They were being helpful, but they were packing things like jars of coffee and plastic crockery that I wasn't going to take with me. "Let me do, let me do," I protested, then packed a few things—letters, some clothes, things like that. I stuffed them all into a traveling bag.

The Warden appeared and stood watching me. "Be quick! Be quick!"

I was beyond being upset. It was like a dream in which I was carried peacefully along.

When I appeared at the door of the building, packed and ready, all the people I'd come to love were standing at the foot of the steps—Jenny, Chris, Su, and the others. The Thai prisoners were standing a little farther away, because the Warden was watching. I took each of my friends in my arms one by one. I thought my heart would break, leaving them behind. I hugged Jenny the longest. She had the worst sentence, and that made the various frictions we'd had seem irrelevant.

The Warden moved me along. I was smiling radiantly. At the end of the line stood Hannah: Hannah, with whom I had been on bad terms for several months, ever since our row over my newspaper publicity. I was suddenly confused, not knowing how to speak to her now that I was leaving.

She was saying good-bye. I heard her words of farewell but couldn't respond. She was too bound up with Lard Yao. Hannah had always been the one you could rely on to get a favor for you from the Warden. She knew the system. She made it work for her. Seeing her standing there, I realized that, in many ways, she was the prison. It was her life.

I felt pity . . . contempt . . . a mixture of conflicting emotions. I looked into her eyes and could not read what I saw there. In the end I gave up trying to find something to say. I left Hannah without a word, passing silently by her words of farewell.

It seemed a long walk to the prison gates. One of the guards carried my bag. As we walked past one of the buildings, Mary and Linda shouted down to me. "Wow! Great! Good luck, Rita!" The Warden glared up at them. "Who's making that noise? Be quiet! Stop it at once!" From the factory, as we passed, came cheers from some of the Thai prisoners.

We were at the gate, and the moment I had dreamed of for nearly three years was actually happening. I walked through the small door cut into the gate. I stood on the dusty road. In all that long walk from the dormitory steps, I had not turned around once.

I was put into a van with two junior guards. It had been used not long before to take a woman to her execution. The Warden watched me get in. Nearby stood the one high-ranking official who had been genuinely kind to me. Crying, I pushed open the van window.

"I'm going out," I sobbed. "For three years I was in there. And you were the only one who was good to me. . . ."

In the van, I realized I was still holding a pair of earrings I'd intended to give to Jenny. I gave them to one of the junior guards, asking her to give them to Jenny later. The Warden peered into the cab. "Hurry! Hurry!" The engine coughed into life. We drove away.

For about fifteen minutes we drove through heavy traffic. Then the van pulled up by the roadside.

"Get out," said one of the guards. I clambered down. The guard tossed my bag after me. "Bye, bye! Write to us!" I watched the vehicle lumber off, back the way we had come.

I had no idea what was happening. I hadn't imagined that it would be like this—dumped on the side of the road. Too happy to be frightened, but very confused, I began praying. "Lord, please help me." I picked up my bag and started walking. Almost immediately, I came to a small police station. I walked in. There was a policeman on duty.

"Hello," I announced. "I'm Rita Nightingale. May I use your phone?"

24   Home

*I am Rita Nightingale, and I have
been reborn again.*

Interview with David Allin, *Lancashire
Evening Telegraph*, January 24, 1980

The police were very friendly. "Hey! Look at this!"
they joked. "Nice-looking foreigner who speaks
Thai. You want a Coke, something to eat maybe?"

"I want to use the telephone," I insisted.

"Oh, sure," they agreed and waved me over to the
phone. I was clutching Mr. Coleshill's card. I dialed
the number. The phone was temperamental, and I
was still dialing and re-dialing when one of the
policemen tapped me on the shoulder."

"Are you Rita?"

He pointed to another phone, with its receiver off the hook. "For you," he said laconically.

It was Mr. Puttri. "Rita? Now, listen. Stay exactly where you are. Don't move from the police station; don't go anywhere until we come. We have been told that you were being brought there. We are on our way."

I put the phone back. Somebody gave me a Coke and I began to relax. The police joked with me. "My, you're a pretty girl to be speaking Thai!"

"Well," I countered cheerfully, "you're not so bad-looking yourself." We bantered for a few minutes. I felt lightheaded and very happy.

There was a shout from the road. I went to the front and looked out. Mr. Coleshill, the Consul, was standing outside. He hugged me, and for the next few minutes we talked nonstop.

I am so grateful to him. He was always very proper in his dealings with my case, and in every way he provided the assistance that anyone would look for from a Consul when in trouble abroad. But the care and support he gave me and the way he sheltered me during those first few days of freedom went far beyond the demands of duty. In the news photographs taken at the time he is nearly always to be seen, well out of the limelight but always near at hand.

Then Mr. Puttri arrived—dear Mr. Puttri, who had worked so hard on my case and had as often as not had little thanks from me in return. I don't know what he did for me, because he was always speaking Thai in court, but I know he was regarded as a fine lawyer, and he was very kind to me. He brought Leonie with him. She had brought me a fresh strawberry, which was a real treat at that time in Bangkok.

I was leaping up and down joyfully, tremendously excited, praising the Lord and unable to believe what had happened. Mr. Coleshill stayed protectively close and must have felt as if he were escorting a whirling dervish.

Officially, I had to report to the Immigration Office, but Mr. Coleshill had insisted that I be allowed to go to the Embassy first. When we walked through the door, another world I'd forgotten confronted me. Wallpaper . . . carpet . . . a chair. . . . People greeted me pleasantly, but I was staring open-mouthed at everything.

Mr. Coleshill winked at me conspiratorially. "Now," he beamed. "I've something rather special you'll enjoy."

He took me down a corridor and opened a door. "Just stay in there as long as you like," he said. It was a bathroom. It had a European toilet, pink wallpaper and tiles, and a mirror. The people in the Embassy must have wondered what the wild shout of joy was that came from the bathroom as I rushed in joyfully. For at least fifteen minutes I luxuriated in the opulence of a Western bathroom, flushing the toilet, turning the taps, looking at myself in the mirror; I couldn't believe it.

Eventually Mr. Coleshill took me, clean and glowing, to Immigration. As we arrived, an enormous crowd of reporters from different countries surged forward with cameras and tape recorders. Mr. Coleshill squared his shoulders. "We'll get you through this somehow," he promised.

We began to make our way through. I felt no tension. There was a clearing in the crowd. I saw dear Mr. Lyman standing there. He had, I found out later, been waiting there for me since I'd left the police station.

His sight had deteriorated in the time I'd known him. Now he peered anxiously in my direction. I flew into his arms and hugged and kissed him. He gripped my shoulders and laughed with me. "We did it, li'l honey! I *knew* we'd do it! I knew we would!" He whirled me around, and we shouted joyfully.

It was getting dark. I was being moved on to the offices. I held Mr. Lyman a moment longer. "I'll do my best to see you again before I go," I vowed.

Albert Lyman had been my lawyer from the beginning. He had put up with my bitterness and anger. For nearly three years he had championed my case, and for most of the time he had no help from me. I owe more to him and his firm than I can say, and I was so glad to see him there.

In Immigration, Mr. Coleshill asked me, "Now, Rita. Do you feel able to talk to the reporters?"

"Sure!" I said happily. I was still on cloud nine.

"Be very careful," he advised. "Don't be led into saying anything you don't want to say."

I can't remember anything I said. I do remember that in my dazed state the hardest thing was to construct English sentences. I'd been among Thai speakers for so long. My accent had become very peculiar. "I thought you were English!" remarked one reporter.

Somebody asked me who I would like to say thank you to. It was quite a question to be asked in my state, but I tried to list everybody. I ended up repeating over and over, "I want to thank God.... I want to thank him for everything he's done in my life. I want to thank all the Christians who have been praying for me." I saw Mr. Puttri glancing nervously at me. I remembered just in time. "And I want to thank the King for pardoning me."

I was truly grateful to His Majesty the King of Thailand, and I still am. I am well aware that though amnesties for lesser offenses are a traditional feature of the Thai royal calendar, the act of clemency shown to me, who had been found guilty of smuggling drugs, risked international criticism as fierce as that which had followed my arrest. Whether it was a personal intervention on his part or a decision made at the ministry level, I am deeply grateful to His Majesty King Bhumibol. At that moment, however, I was so thrilled by God's goodness to me that somehow my answer to the questioner came out rather one-sided.

Mr. Puttri and Mr. Coleshill accompanied me into Immigration. It was the same office where I had been arrested. Some police were there, but there were no big guns to be seen, just small arms carried in shoulder holsters such as all Thai police wear.

There was a big discussion about where I was to sleep that night. I gathered from what was being said to Mr. Coleshill in Thai that I would not be permitted to sleep in the Embassy. I didn't mind. A girl who'd been released from Lard Yao a few days earlier was being detained in Immigration while some details were sorted out. "Get me in with Rosemary," I assured Mr. Coleshill, "and I won't mind sleeping in a cell."

So I ended up in a cell with Rosemary, sharing it with a number of Khmer refugees from Cambodia.

It was quite noisy, but my meeting with Rosemary was noisier. "I couldn't believe it when I saw it in the papers!" she screamed.

Mr. Coleshill was allowed to see me in the cell. "I know I can't get you out tonight," he said, "but I can bring you anything you want to eat."

"I want a steak!" I cried ecstatically. "And I want a salad and a cold drink, and I want a baked potato . . . ." Mr. Coleshill went off to get it.

Later a guard called me to the door. To my surprise he dumped a suitcase at my feet. "For you."

I opened it. On the top was a press photograph from the *Daily Mail*, showing my mother and my sister Ann raising champagne glasses to the camera. They had obviously heard the news. There was also a letter from Mother, brief but heartfelt. She mentioned that Ian Smith of the *Daily Mail* was in Bangkok. On my behalf Mom had accepted the paper's offer of help to get me home. She explained that I wasn't bound to say anything to anybody and that if I didn't want to, I didn't even have to meet Mr. Smith.

I barely took the details in. I stared at the photograph. My heart was full. Up to that moment, the whirlwind of events had pushed my family to one side of my thoughts. Now, looking at the photograph, I knew I wanted to go home.

By the time Mr. Coleshill arrived with the feast, I had pulled myself together. Rosemary and I sat down and ate and ate. We tried to share the food with the refugees, but they didn't know what it was and wouldn't eat any. I couldn't resist trying a bit of everything; it had been so long since I'd had that sort of food. I paid a price for it later though. My insides were churning around for days, and I was forever having to leave important meetings suddenly. . . .

I wanted to shower before I left. The shower was actually private; it was possible to wash without an audience. But as soon as I was inside, I was transfixed by fear. It took a few minutes for me to realize that the fear was because for the first time in three years, I was in a dark place. There had been nowhere really dark in the prison. In the end, I had to ask Rosemary to stay with me and keep me company while I showered.

Next morning a number of people came to the cell to see me, and then I went to the Immigration offices. As I went down the steps, I saw Gladys Martin. We ran to each other. "Oh!" she exclaimed. "I'm so glad to see you!" She had been refused permission to see me earlier and had decided to wait there until I went past. My time with her was all too brief. In no time at all I was in Immigration, being asked innumerable routine questions and being put through the proper procedures. There were scores of photographers. For the first time I became irritated as I was pulled this way and that as they all competed for photographs of what was happening. Mr. Coleshill efficiently made sure that I wasn't overwhelmed.

"I've got permission for you to have an hour or two free—you can rest in my apartment," he told me afterward. "There'll be a couple of police standing by, but don't worry about that."

As we drove through Bangkok, I stared like a child at everything we passed. On the way, we stopped at Mr. Lyman's house and stayed with him and his wife for half an hour.

"Please visit us at home when you come to England," I begged.

"I don't think I'll ever make that journey again," he said regretfully. "I'm getting to be an old man, li'l honey."

And so we said good-bye to each other.

Mr. Coleshill's apartment was blessedly free from photographers. I washed my hair, glorying in the luxury of that splendid bathroom. As I emerged, damp and very happy, there was a knock on the door. "You open it," said Mr. Coleshill. I did. Lucille was standing there.

During all my time in prison she had visited me faithfully, supporting me, encouraging my mother, caring for me in thousands of ways; and this was the first time I had been close enough to touch her. I was overwhelmed. As I was recovering from the excitement, Jack and Gladys arrived, bringing Margaret Cole with them. Then one by one other people who had played a part in the whole story came in: Mr. Lyman, Canon Taylor, and several others. It was wonderful; I hadn't expected anything like it. The meal we had together was a lovely, precious celebration.

It had to finish eventually. It seemed hardly any time had gone by before I was saying good-bye to everybody. Lucille and Margaret and Jack and Gladys prayed with me for the last time, and I shared with them my hopes and fears for the future. The euphoria was beginning to fade, as I realized I would soon be back in England. "I don't know any Christians there," I told Jack. "I don't know which church to go to or anything like that."

"You'll be all right," he replied. "The Lord has his hand on your life, we know that. He is going to protect you and use you."

The emotional distress of saying good-bye to my friends showed when I got upset with photographers a little later. After guiding me through that unpleasant session, Mr. Coleshill said, "We have to decide what you're going to do, Rita. You must leave Bangkok today. Where would you like to go?"

I believe God guided me very clearly then. "Mr. Coleshill, there's nothing I want more than to go home and be with my mother and my family. But I can't go straight home. I want to go to Kuala Lumpur, to sort myself out and settle down."

Doctors working with freed hostages and prisoners now insist that the captive should go through an interim period of adjustment before being allowed to go home. I didn't know about this "hostage psychology," but I believe God planted that instinctive decision in my mind to protect me from emotional problems which would otherwise have spoiled my homecoming.

We went to the airport in the best James Bond-style to avoid publicity (rather spoiled by my discovery that the bag I was carrying, a present from a friend, bore my name in bold letters for any passer-by to see!). We got there with a minimum of fuss. However, as we emerged from a lift, Ian Smith of the *Daily Mail* and a photographer were standing waiting to enter. "It's her!" they exclaimed, and so the *Mail* got a scoop photograph.

I traveled first class to Kuala Lumpur. When I stepped down from the plane, I saw groups of

Europeans waiting for their flights. I froze.

"What's the matter?" asked Mr. Coleshill.

"All those people!" I said. "They're so big. . . ." I had grown accustomed to Easterners, who are on the average much shorter than Westerners.

Mr. Coleshill, who was staying at the Embassy, left me at the hotel with strict instructions to answer the door to nobody but himself and to speak to nobody who telephoned. I hung the "Do not disturb" sign on the door, shut and locked it, and sat down.

Immediately, an indescribable fear swept over me. I couldn't handle it; I knelt down and prayed. *Lord, what is this feeling? What's happening?*

And then I realized what it was. I was alone.

For nearly three years I hadn't experienced quiet and solitude. I had already faced the dark, but this was much more of a shock. I was alone with myself, and it was quiet.

When I realized what the fear was, I rejoiced and praised God. Now I knew that I was free.

Nevertheless, I wasn't used to it. I opened the window to let the traffic noise in and curled up on the soft bed with the radio on quietly to give a background noise. But I couldn't sleep. I tossed and turned. It wasn't the heat—the hotel air-conditioning was bliss after Lard Yao's sticky nights. It was the softness of the bed. In the end I got out of bed and curled up on the floor and so, managed to doze.

I persuaded Mr. Coleshill to let me visit the hotel shop next day. I bought some candy and wandered away to stand at the edge of the hotel pool, watching a crowd of bronzed swimmers. I was laughing to myself out of sheer happiness. I kept thinking about Jenny and Hannah and all the others, but I had to push the thoughts out of my mind. I wasn't capable of handling them—there was so much going on in my head.

Behind me, Mr. Coleshill was urging, "Come on! Get back inside the hotel!"

"Oh, please let me stay," I implored him. "Nobody's going to recognize me."

"With hair like that?" He pointed at my long, wild hair. "Everybody will recognize you! Come inside!"

We drove to the home of a lady from the Foreign Office for lunch. She was really lovely to me. When I sat down at the beautifully appointed luncheon table, I broke down and had to leave the room. It was an hour before I could return. I had never seen anything so lovely.

These stages were all important, and I'm still glad that I asked Mr. Coleshill if I could have that period of adjustment. But now I was beginning to want to go home.

I knew that Ian Smith had flown to Kuala Lumpur, and I decided to contact him. I didn't have to speak to any reporter if I didn't want to, Mr. Coleshill pointed out, but the *Daily Mail* had offered me a flight home. I arranged to meet Ian Smith at the airport. Mr. Coleshill wasn't able to take me there, so we said our good-byes at the house where we'd had lunch. He was reassuring and kind, just as he had been all the time since I left prison. I will always be grateful to him. I have many debts of gratitude I will never be able to repay, but he was special. I don't know how I would have managed for those first few days without him.

On the plane we sat in the first-class lounge, which was virtually empty. Ian Smith explained that there was no need to talk if I didn't want to. He would even go and sit on the other side of the lounge if I wanted to sleep all the way home.

"Well," I suggested, not wanting to seem ungrateful, "we could always have a cup of tea together, couldn't we?"

As we sipped our tea, something seemed to unlock inside me, and I poured out the story of my life to him, right from the beginning, the bad and the good things. I talked for hours about my childhood, my family, James, the arrest, Hannah, Jenny, Maria—all of it. I talked about Jesus and what he had done for me; about Valerie, and Mary, and Linda. I shared my hopes and my fears. It all tumbled out, and Ian Smith listened patiently. Only a tiny fraction of what I said ever found its way into print. Ian Smith was kind and understanding with me, and I'm sure that my telling him everything was another necessary stage in my return to the outside world. God was guiding me step by step, providing me with the right people to help me at each stage.

I knew that there would be crowds at London Airport. Paul McCartney was returning the same day after his arrest in Japan on drug charges. When I looked out of the plane as we landed, I saw a crowd of reporters.

"It's this plane they're waiting for, not McCartney's," smiled Ian Smith. However, it was at least twenty minutes before I felt able to leave my seat. I was shaking with fright. It wasn't the reporters. It was the overwhelming knowledge that I was home at last. The nightmare was over.

Eventually a police superintendent came on

board— a solid, friendly, unarmed London police-man.

"Are you all right, love?"

"I'm OK. . . . I just can't get up. . . . I can't leave the plane."

He was very understanding. "Look, love. Those are your friends out there. They're all on your side. But just in case, I've got 200 of my boys waiting to see you through to the airport lounge. And your Uncle George Nightingale is waiting for you around the corner."

I stood up, suddenly calm. I went down the steps, pushed past the reporters, and made my way through the crowd.

The policeman walking by my side murmured, "Just keep walking. . . . Keep walking. You'll be all right."

And then at the end of the runway I saw my Uncle George, who had come to greet me and take me to my mother and sisters. He looked beautiful with his gleaming white hair and a broad smile on his face.

I started running toward him, forgetting the crowds, forgetting the police and reporters. I opened my arms wide and raced across to him, crying and laughing at the same time. I half fell, half collapsed, into his arms, into his embrace, into the rest of my life.

Postscript

Several weeks after my release Lucille sent me a press cutting. Maria had been called to the Supreme Court for sentencing. The newspaper photo showed her barefooted and bewildered outside a court cell; the court had ordered her release. She was to be sent back to Spain.

Hannah, Jenny, and Chris are still in Lard Yao, serving their sentences.

Linda and Mary are still going through the court hearings at the time of this writing. It will be some months before they know their sentences.

Three months after my return, my mother asked Jesus into her life. She was fifty-eight, fit, active, and very happy to have me back home after such a long absence. Several weeks after she became a Christian, she fell ill, and died within three months. I don't know why God allowed her to die, but I am so grateful to him for those months I spent nursing her. It was the best time I ever had with her.

Sometime after Mother's death, I went to America. I had been invited by the Prison Fellowship, the group started by Chuck Colson, which I had first heard about in Lard Yao. After visiting me in Bangkok, Kathryn Grant had reported back to the Fellowship, and they had begun to pray for me with a new urgency. They were thrilled when they heard that, only weeks after Kathryn's visit, I had been released. I spent two months with the Fellowship and returned to England with a growing sense that my own experiences in prison could be used by God in reaching other prisoners. In January 1981, I joined the staff of Prison Christian Fellowship, the daughter organization in Britain. Since then I have worked for this ministry to prison inmates and their families. So, my own concern for other prisoners and the prophecy Margaret Cole made to the King of Thailand about my future have been fulfilled.

My work takes me into prisons and reformatories all over Britain. I share my prison experiences and the love of God with the inmates. I also go to churches and fellowship groups, encouraging them to pray for inmates, as well as for Christians to become more involved with the prisons.

In the course of this book I have been able to say thank-you to many people. There are still many more who helped and encouraged me in numerous ways during the events described, and for various reasons they do not appear. Some of them I will never know about, so I am grateful to be able to take this opportunity of publicly thanking each one of them.

Other Living Books Bestsellers

THE BEST CHRISTMAS PAGEANT EVER by Barbara Robinson. A delightfully wild and funny story about what can happen to a Christmas program when the "horrible Herdman" family of brothers and sisters are miscast in the roles of the Christmas story characters from the Bible. 07-0137 $2.50.

ELIJAH by William H. Stephens. He was a rough-hewn farmer who strolled onto the stage of history to deliver warnings to Ahab the king and to defy Jezebel the queen. A powerful biblical novel you will never forget. 07-4023 $3.50.

THE TOTAL MAN by Dan Benson. A practical guide on how to gain confidence and fulfillment. Covering areas such as budgeting of time, money matters, and marital relationships. 07-7289 $3.50.

HOW TO HAVE ALL THE TIME YOU NEED EVERY DAY by Pat King. Drawing from her own and other women's experiences as well as from the Bible and the research of time experts, Pat has written a warm and personal book for every Christian woman. 07-1529 $2.95.

IT'S INCREDIBLE by Ann Kiemel. "It's incredible" is what some people say when a slim young woman says, "Hi. I'm Ann," and starts talking about love and good and beauty. As Ann tells about a Jesus who can make all the difference in their lives, some call that incredible, and turn away. Others become miracles themselves, agreeing with Ann that it's incredible. 07-1818 $2.50.

EVERGREEN CASTLES by Laurie Clifford. A heartwarming story about the growing pains of five children whose hilarious adventures teach them unforgettable lessons about love and forgiveness, life and death. Delightful reading for all ages. 07-0779 $2.95.

JOHN, SON OF THUNDER by Ellen Gunderson Traylor. Travel with John down the desert paths, through the courts of the Holy City, and to the foot of the cross. Journey with him from his luxury as a privileged son of Israel to the bitter hardship of his exile on Patmos. This is a saga of adventure, romance, and discovery—of a man bigger than life—the disciple "whom Jesus loved." 07-1903 $3.95.

WHAT'S IN A NAME? compiled by Linda Francis, John Hartzel, and Al Palmquist. A fascinating name dictionary that features the literal meaning of people's first names, the character quality implied by the name, and an applicable Scripture verse for each name listed. Ideal for expectant parents! 07-7935 $2.95.

Other Living Books Bestsellers

DAVID AND BATHSHEBA by Roberta Kells Dorr. Was Bathsheba an innocent country girl or a scheming adulteress? What was King David really like? Solomon—the wisest man in the world—was to be king, but could he survive his brothers' intrigues? Here is an epic love story which comes radiantly alive through the art of a fine storyteller. 07-0618 $3.95.

TOO MEAN TO DIE by Nick Pirovolos with William Proctor. In this action-packed story, Nick the Greek tells how he grew from a scrappy immigrant boy to a fearless underworld criminal. Finally caught, he was imprisoned. But something remarkable happened and he was set free—truly set free! 07-7283 $3.50.

FOR WOMEN ONLY. This bestseller gives a balanced, entertaining, diversified treatment of all aspects of womanhood. Edited by Evelyn and J. Allan Petersen, founder of Family Concern. 07-0897 $3.50.

FOR MEN ONLY. Edited by J. Allan Petersen, this book gives solid advice on how men can cope with the tremendous pressures they face every day as fathers, husbands, workers. 07-0892 $3.50.

ROCK. What is rock music really doing to you? Bob Larson presents a well-researched and penetrating look at today's rock music and rock performers. What are lyrics really saying? Who are the top performers and what are their life-styles? 07-5686 $2.95.

THE ALCOHOL TRAP by Fred Foster. A successful film executive was about to lose everything—his family's vacation home, his house in New Jersey, his reputation in the film industry, his wife. This is an emotion-packed story of hope and encouragement, offering valuable insights into the troubled world of high pressure living and alcoholism. 07-0078 $2.95.

LET ME BE A WOMAN. Best selling author Elisabeth Elliot (author of *THROUGH GATES OF SPLENDOR*) presents her profound and unique perspective on womanhood. This is a significant book on a continuing controversial subject. 07-2162 $2.95.

WE'RE IN THE ARMY NOW by Imeldia Morris Eller. Five children become their older brother's "army" as they work together to keep their family intact during a time of crisis for their mother. 07-7862 $2.95.

WILD CHILD by Mari Hanes. A heartrending story of a young boy who was abandoned and struggled alone for survival. You will be moved as you read how one woman's love tamed this boy who was more animal than human. 07-0223 $2.95.

THE SURGEON'S FAMILY by David Hernandez with Carole Gift Page. This is an incredible three-generation story of a family that has faced danger and death—and has survived. Walking dead-end streets of violence and poverty, often seemingly without hope, the family of David Hernandez has struggled to find a new kind of life. 07-6684 $2.95.

Other Living Books Bestsellers

THE MAN WHO COULD DO NO WRONG by Charles E. Blair with John and Elizabeth Sherrill. He built one of the largest churches in America . . . then he made a mistake. This is the incredible story of Pastor Charles E. Blair, accused of massive fraud. A book "for error-prone people in search of the Christian's secret for handling mistakes." 07-4002 $3.50.

GIVERS, TAKERS AND OTHER KINDS OF LOVERS by Josh McDowell. This book bypasses vague generalities about love and sex and gets right down to basic questions: Whatever happened to sexual freedom? What's true love like? What is your most important sex organ? Do men respond differently than women? If you're looking for straight answers about God's plan for love and sexuality then this book was written for you. 07-1023 $2.50.

MORE THAN A CARPENTER by Josh McDowell. This best selling author thought Christians must be "out of their minds." He put them down. He argued against their faith. But eventually he saw that his arguments wouldn't stand up. In this book, Josh focuses upon the person who changed his life—Jesus Christ. 07-4552 $2.50.

HIND'S FEET ON HIGH PLACES by Hannah Hurnard. A classic allegory which has sold more than a million copies! 07-1429 $3.50.

THE CATCH ME KILLER by Bob Erler with John Souter. Golden gloves, black belt, green beret, silver badge. Supercop Bob Erler had earned the colors of manhood. Now can he survive prison life? An incredible true story of forgiveness and hope. 07-0214 $3.50.

WHAT WIVES WISH THEIR HUSBANDS KNEW ABOUT WOMEN by Dr. James Dobson. By the best selling author of *DARE TO DISCIPLINE* and *THE STRONG-WILLED CHILD,* here's a vital book that speaks to the unique emotional needs and aspirations of today's woman. An immensely practical, interesting guide. 07-7896 $2.95.

PONTIUS PILATE by Dr. Paul Maier. This fascinating novel is about one of the most famous Romans in history—the man who declared Jesus innocent but who nevertheless sent him to the cross. This powerful biblical novel gives you a unique insight into the life and death of Jesus. 07-4852 $3.50.

BROTHER OF THE BRIDE by Donita Dyer. This exciting sequel to *THE BRIDE'S ESCAPE* tells of the faith of a proud, intelligent Armenian family whose Christian heritage stretched back for centuries. A story of suffering, separation, valor, victory, and reunion. 07-0179 $2.95.

LIFE IS TREMENDOUS by Charlie Jones. Believing that enthusiasm makes the difference, Jones shows how anyone can be happy, involved, relevant, productive, healthy, and secure in the midst of a high-pressure, commercialized, automated society. 07-2184 $2.50.

HOW TO BE HAPPY THOUGH MARRIED by Dr. Tim LaHaye. One of America's most successful marriage counselors gives practical, proven advice for marital happiness. 07-1499 $2.95.

The books listed are available at your bookstore. If unavailable, send check with order to cover retail price plus 10% for postage and handling to:

Tyndale House Publishers, Inc.
Box 80
Wheaton, Illinois 60189

Prices and availability subject to change without notice. Allow 4-6 weeks for delivery.